to my parents, Gudrun and Rudolf - P.H.

to Jungwon - F.S.

Actors in Scala

Actors in Scala

Philipp Haller, Frank Sommers

artima

ARTIMA PRESS
WALNUT CREEK, CALIFORNIA

Actors in Scala

Philipp Haller is a post-doctoral researcher at Stanford University, USA, and
EPFL, Switzerland. Frank Sommers is president of Autospaces, Inc.

Artima Press is an imprint of Artima, Inc.
P.O. Box 305, Walnut Creek, California 94597

PrePrint™ Edition first published 2010
First edition published 2011
Build date of this impression December 23, 2011
Produced in the United States of America

15 14 13 12 11   1 2 3 4 5

ISBN-10: 0-9815316-5-2
ISBN-13: 978-0-9815316-5-6

Library of Congress Control Number: 2010911207

Overview

Contents   ix
List of Figures   xii
List of Listings   xiii
Foreword   xvii
Acknowledgments   xix
Introduction   xxi
1. Concurrency Everywhere   3
2. Messages All the Way Up   15
3. Scala's Language Support for Actors   31
4. Actor Chat   45
5. Event-Based Programming   55
6. Exceptions, Actor Termination, and Shutdown   71
7. Customizing Actor Execution   85
8. Remote Actors   101
9. Distributed and Parallel Computing   107
10. Akka Actors   125
11. API Overview   145
Bibliography   159
About the Authors   161
Index   163

Contents

Contents   ix

List of Figures   xii

List of Listings   xiii

Foreword   xvii

Acknowledgments   xix

Introduction   xxi

1 Concurrency Everywhere   3
    1.1   A shift toward parallel hardware   4
    1.2   Actors versus threads   5
    1.3   Scalability   6
    1.4   A high-level perspective on concurrency   7
    1.5   The indeterministic soda machine   9
    1.6   Programming the data center 11

2 Messages All the Way Up   15
    2.1   Control flow and data flow 15
    2.2   Actors and messages 19
    2.3   Actor creation 23
    2.4   Actor events 24
    2.5   Asynchronous communication 27
    2.6   You've got mail: indeterminacy and the role of the arbiter 28
    2.7   Actor life cycle 30

3 Scala's Language Support for Actors   **31**
   3.1 A scalable language   31
   3.2 Immutable and mutable state   33
   3.3 Methods and classes   33
   3.4 First-class functions   34
   3.5 Functions as control structures   36
   3.6 Pattern matching and case classes   41

4 Actor Chat   **45**
   4.1 Defining message classes   46
   4.2 Processing messages   46
   4.3 Sending actor messages   49

5 Event-Based Programming   **55**
   5.1 Events versus threads   55
   5.2 Making actors event-based: `react`   56
   5.3 Event-based futures   65

6 Exceptions, Actor Termination, and Shutdown   **71**
   6.1 Simple exception handling   71
   6.2 Monitoring actors   74

7 Customizing Actor Execution   **85**
   7.1 Pluggable schedulers   85
   7.2 Managed blocking   94

8 Remote Actors   **101**
   8.1 Creating remote actors   101
   8.2 Remote communication   103
   8.3 A remote start service   104

9 Distributed and Parallel Computing   **107**
   9.1 MapReduce   107
   9.2 Reliable broadcast   118

10 Akka Actors   **125**
   10.1 Creating Akka actors   125
   10.2 `ActorRefs`   127
   10.3 Inter-actor interaction, interactively   128

10.4   Message handling 129

10.5   Remote actors in Akka 135

11 API Overview   **145**

11.1   The actor traits `Reactor`, `ReplyReactor`, and `Actor` . .   145

11.2   Control structures   151

11.3   Futures   153

11.4   Channels   154

11.5   Remote Actors API   156

Bibliography   **159**

About the Authors   **161**

Index   **163**

List of Figures

1.1   State transitions in a soda machine.   9
1.2   Message passing with indeterministic message ordering.   . .   11

2.1   Components holding shared state require synchronization.   .   16
2.2   Interaction of data and control flow.   18
2.3   The simplest actor computation: adding x and y together. . .   20
2.4   Actor computation with continuation message passing.   . . .   20
2.5   Every message carries a sender reference.   21
2.6   CruiseControl actor receiving currentSpeed message. . .   21
2.7   A more modular approach to cruise control with further decom-
       position of responsibilities into actors.   22
2.8   A throttleControl continuation included in a message. . .   22
2.9   Creating and delegating work to child actors.   24
2.10   B's arrival event activates C's arrival event.   25
2.11   Event causality in an actor system.   26

4.1   An actor chat application.   45
4.2   Message communication between chat room and users. . . .   47

9.1   Data flow in a basic MAPREDUCE implementation.   115

List of Listings

3.1   Extending `HttpServlet` from Scala   34
3.2   Implementation of the `txn` control structure   38

4.1   Case classes for `Users` and messages.   46
4.2   Defining `act`.   47
4.3   Incoming message patterns.   48
4.4   Creating and starting an actor with `actor`   49
4.5   Representing a user as an actor inside a session   50
4.6   Using the `sender` reference   51
4.7   Using the `reply` method   52
4.8   Using message timeouts with `receiveWithin`   53
4.9   Processing post messages   54

5.1   Building a chain of event-based actors.   57
5.2   The `main` method.   58
5.3   Incorrect use of `react`.   61
5.4   Correct use of `react`.   61
5.5   Sequencing `react` calls using a recursive method.   62
5.6   A `sleep` method that uses `react`.   63
5.7   Using `andThen` to continue after `react`.   63
5.8   Using `loopWhile` for iterations with `react`.   64
5.9   Image renderer using futures.   65
5.10 Using `react` to wait for futures.   67
5.11 Enabling `react` in `for` expressions.   68
5.12 Implementing the custom `ForEach` operator.   68

6.1   Defining an actor-global exception handler.   72
6.2   Linking dependent actors.   76

6.3	Receiving a notification because of an unhandled exception.	79
6.4	Monitoring and restarting an actor using link and restart.	81
6.5	Using keepAlive to automatically restart a crashed actor. .	82
6.6	Reacting to Exit messages for exception handling.	83
7.1	Incorrect use of ThreadLocal.	88
7.2	Saving and restoring a ThreadLocal.	88
7.3	Executing actors on the Swing event dispatch thread.	90
7.4	Creating daemon-style actors.	91
7.5	Synchronizing the speed of Gear actors.	92
7.6	Blocked actors may lock up the thread pool.	95
7.7	Using managed blocking to prevent thread-pool lock up. . .	97
8.1	Making the chat room actor remotely accessible.	102
8.2	A server actor implementing a remote start service.	105
8.3	An echo actor that you can start remotely.	106
9.1	A function for building an inverted index.	109
9.2	A basic MAPREDUCE implementation.	112
9.3	Applying the reducing function in parallel.	114
9.4	A MAPREDUCE implementation that tolerates mapper faults.	116
9.5	MAPREDUCE with coarse-grained worker tasks.	119
9.6	Best-effort broadcasting.	120
9.7	Using the broadcast implementation in user code.	121
9.8	A reliable broadcast actor.	123
9.9	Sending messages with time stamps.	123
10.1	A simple chain actor in Akka.	126
10.2	A master actor controlling an actor chain.	129
10.3	Using become to implement a simple unbounded buffer. . .	132
10.4	A consumer interacting with the buffer.	133
10.5	A buffer actor that handles both Put and Get messages. . .	134
10.6	The MasterService object.	136
10.7	The MasterService actor.	137
10.8	The ClusterService object.	139
10.9	The ClusterService actor.	140
10.10	A simple actor that you can start remotely.	141
11.1	Using andThen for sequencing.	152

11.2 Scope-based sharing of channels.   155
11.3 Sharing channels via messages.   156

Foreword

I have been fascinated by concurrency and distributed computing for as long as I can remember. I still remember the joy of solving the classic dining philosophers problem using my own semaphore library built on top of the pthreads C library back in university many years ago. A few years later a new language called Java came along. Java made a lot of things easier for us developers; it had, for example, automatic memory management and a rich standard library. It also came with a single unified abstraction over threads and had concurrency utilities built into the language (for example, `wait`, `notify`, and `synchronized`), which was later expanded with the rich `java.util.concurrent` library. I embraced Java as my primary language of choice. The problem was that writing concurrent programs still needed too much low-level plumbing and was still way too hard. The main reason for this was that Java blindly adopted the C/C++ concurrency paradigm; shared-state concurrency, *e.g.*, concurrent access to shared mutable state, which in most cases is not what you need and therefore the wrong default.

Over the years I have done my share of programming with threads and locks, spending late nights and weekends at the office tracking down concurrency bugs. One day I just had enough. I started reading up on alternative concurrency paradigms, in particular message-passing concurrency as implemented by the language and runtime Erlang, and dataflow concurrency from an esoteric academic language called Oz. I was amazed by both of these languages and their approach to concurrency; in particular, Erlang and its actor-based programming model. Actors raised the abstraction level from threads and locks and made it so much easier to write, understand, and maintain my concurrent code. Instead of spending time getting the plumbing right, I could focus on the workflow—how the messages flowed in the system— which made my code so much easier to understand and maintain. So I fell in love with Erlang and its actors. Actors also turned out to be great not only for concurrency but also for fault tolerance and distributed computing. I had finally found a tool that I could use to scale up, utilizing symmetric multiprocessor (SMP)/multicore machines, scale out on the cluster, and write highly available systems. Life was good.

About five years ago I discovered and fell in love with Scala. In Scala, I found a fascinating language that blended object-oriented and functional programming with rare elegance, ran on the JVM, was statically typed with the same performance as Java, and...had actors. It couldn't be better. All the goodness of Erlang on the JVM. I started using Scala and Scala's actors as my main language and tool set for writing scalable, fault-tolerant, and highly concurrent systems. This eventually led me to create Akka, an actor runtime that builds upon the Scala foundation by adding even richer tools for concurrency and distributed computing.

I have a lot to thank Philipp Haller, one of the two authors of this book and the creator of Scala actors. Without his excellent work I would probably not have started using Scala and would not have created Akka. I would have missed out on a lot of fun. I am really glad that Philipp and Frank have taken the time to write this book. Now we finally have an introductory book that teaches how to use actors in Scala and that covers both Scala's actors library as well as Akka. It is a great first step into the wonderful world of actors. See reading this book as an investment: it will help you to write correct, performant, scalable, and available systems in less time, giving more time to more important things in life.

Jonas Bonér
CTO Typesafe
Uppsala, Sweden
November 1, 2011

Acknowledgments

There are many people who have shaped this book in different ways. First and foremost, we'd like to thank Tom Van Cutsem for contributing large parts of Chapter 9 ("Distributed and Parallel Computing"); at least half of the material on MAPREDUCE was contributed by him. In the same chapter, the solutions for best-effort and reliable broadcast are based on code contributed by Aleksandar Prokopec.

We are grateful to Kunle Olukotun and Martin Odersky for supporting Philipp's work on this book in 2011, while being a post-doctoral research fellow at Stanford University, USA, and at École Polytechnique Fédérale de Lausanne (EPFL), Switzerland.

We'd also like to thank Stéphane Micheloud, Samira Tasharofi, Mirco Dotta, and Vojin Jovanovic, for reviewing earlier versions and preprints of this book. Their feedback has helped us improve the text in countless places.

Special thanks go to Bill Venners who initially came up with the idea of a book on Scala actors. Without his expertise in publishing and his continuous support over many months, this book would not have been possible.

Introduction

This book is a tutorial for programming with actors in the Scala programming language. Actors provide a high-level programming model for concurrent and distributed systems based on lightweight processes and message passing. One of the authors of this book, Philipp Haller, is the creator of Scala's actors library, and is directly involved in the development of actors in Scala's standard library. Our goal is that by reading this book, you can learn everything you need to build efficient, scalable, and robust concurrent software for the JVM, productively, using actors. All examples in this book compile with Scala version 2.9.1 and Akka version 1.2.

Who should read this book

The main target audience of this book is programmers who want to learn how to program using actors in Scala. If you are interested in building highly concurrent, scalable systems in Scala, then this book introduces you to Scala's main offering in this space, actors. This book provides an introduction both to actors in Scala's standard library, as well as to Akka's actors, which enable even more powerful facilities for fault-tolerant event-driven middleware solutions.

In addition, students and programmers who would like to expand their knowledge of concurrent and distributed programming by learning about a not-yet-standard concurrency paradigm should find this book interesting. As a Java programmer, for example, you might be used to programming with threads, synchronized methods, volatile fields, and so on. Learning about actors, and the underlying approach to modeling concurrent systems, can help you think about concurrency differently, thereby broadening your horizons.

Basic programming knowledge in Scala is assumed, as well as some familiarity with virtual machine environments like the JVM or .NET. The book contains a separate chapter which introduces Scala language features that are essential for programming effectively with actors, so you don't have to be an expert (or even intermediate) Scala programmer. In general, we believe this book is a good companion to "Programming in Scala" (also published by Artima, Inc.).

How to use this book

Because the main purpose of this book is to serve as a tutorial, the recommended way to read this book is in chapter order, from front to back. We have tried hard to introduce one topic at a time, and explain new topics only in terms of topics we've already introduced. Thus, if you skip to the back to get an early peek at something, you may find it explained in terms of concepts you don't quite understand. To the extent you read the chapters in order, we think you'll find it quite straightforward to gain competency in Scala actors. After you have read the book once, it should also serve as a reference for Scala actors.

EBook features

This book is available in both paper and PDF eBook form. The eBook is not simply an electronic copy of the paper version of the book. While the content is the same as in the paper version, the eBook has been carefully designed and optimized for reading on a computer screen.

The first thing to notice is that most references within the eBook are hyperlinked. If you select a reference to a chapter, or figure, your PDF viewer should take you immediately to the selected item so that you do not have to flip around to find it.

Additionally, at the bottom of each page in the eBook are a number of navigation links. The "Cover," "Overview," and "Contents" links take you to the front matter of the book. The "Index" link takes you to reference parts of the book. Finally, the "Discuss" link takes you to an online forum where you discuss questions with other readers, the authors, and the larger Scala community. If you find a typo, or something you think could be explained better, please click on the "Suggest" link, which will take you to an online web application where you can give the authors feedback.

Although the same pages appear in the eBook as the printed book, blank pages are removed and the remaining pages renumbered. The pages are numbered differently so that it is easier for you to determine PDF page numbers when printing only a portion of the eBook. The pages in the eBook are, therefore, numbered exactly as your PDF viewer will number them.

Typographic conventions

The first time a *term* is used, it is italicized. Small code examples, such as x + 1, are written inline with a mono-spaced font. Larger code examples are put into mono-spaced quotation blocks like this:

```
def hello() {
  println("Hello, world!")
}
```

When interactive shells are shown, responses from the shell are shown in a lighter font:

```
scala> 3 + 4
res0: Int = 7
```

Content overview

- Chapter 1, "Concurrency Everywhere," gives an overview of actor-based concurrency as well as the reasoning, and history, behind it.

- Chapter 2, "Messages All the Way Up," birds-eye view of the actor programming model refers to features that Scala actors already implement and when relevant, points out differences between Scala actors and the more general model.

- Chapter 3, "Scala's Language Support for Actors," reviews the Scala features most relevant to actors for the Java developer who has little or no experience with Scala.

- Chapter 4, "Actor Chat," illustrates the key elements of Scala's actor DSL with a quintessential messaging application: a chat program.

- Chapter 5, "Event-Based Programming," covers event-based actors which are implemented as event handlers and are more lightweight than their thread-based cousins. This chapter discusses thread pools as an execution environment for event-based actors, as well as event-based futures.

- Chapter 6, "Exceptions, Actor Termination, and Shutdown," covers how to handle errors in concurrent, actor-based programs - handling exceptions, monitoring other actors to detect termination, and termination management of actor-based programs.

- Chapter 7, "Customizing Actor Execution," shows you how to customize the runtime system, improve the integration with threads and thread-local data, simplify testing, and more.

- Chapter 8, "Remote Actors," explains the constructs involved in using remote actors, revisits the chat example application from Chapter 4. You will learn how to create remote actors and how to address and communicate between remote actors.

- Chapter 9, "Distributed and Parallel Computing," illustrates how to accomplish some common parallel and distributed computing tasks with actors focusing on two patterns, MAPREDUCE and reliable broadcasting.

- Chapter 10, "Akka," introduces the essentials of Akka from a user's perspective and explains the main differences to Scala actors, from an operational point of view.

- Chapter 11, "API Overview," provides a detailed API overview of the `scala.actors` package in Scala 2.8 and Scala 2.9. The organization follows groups of types that logically belong together as well as the trait hierarchy.

Resources

At `http://www.scala-lang.org`, the main website for Scala, you'll find the latest Scala release and links to documentation and community resources. For a page of links to resources about Scala and Akka actors, visit this book's website: http://booksites.artima.com/actors_in_scala. To interact with other readers of this book, check out the Actors in Scala Forum, at: http://www.artima.com/forums/forum.jsp?forum=287.

Source code

You can download a ZIP file containing the source code of this book, which is released under the Apache 2.0 open source license, from the book's website: http://booksites.artima.com/actors_in_scala.

Errata

Although this book has been heavily reviewed and checked, errors will inevitably slip through. For a (hopefully short) list of errata for this book, visit http://booksites.artima.com/actors_in_scala/errata.

If you find an error, please report it at the above URL, so that we can be sure to fix it in a future printing or edition of this book.

Actors in Scala

Chapter 1

Concurrency Everywhere

The actor model of concurrency was born of a practical need: When Carl Hewitt and his team at MIT first described actors in the 1970s, computers were relatively slow.[1] While developers could already divide up work among several computers and compute in parallel, Hewitt's team wanted a model that would not only simplify building such concurrent systems, but would also let them reason about concurrent programs in general. Such reasoning, Hewitt and his team believed, would allow developers to be more certain that their concurrent programs worked as intended.

Although actor-based concurrency has been an important concept ever since, it is only now gaining widespread acceptance. That is in part because until recently no widely used programming language offered first-class support for actors. An effective actors implementation places a great burden on a host language, and few mainstream languages were up to the task. Scala rises to that challenge, and offers full-featured implementations of actor-based concurrency on the Java virtual machine (JVM). Because Scala code seamlessly interoperates with code and libraries written in Java, and other languages for the JVM, Scala-based actors offer an exciting and practical way to build scalable and reliable concurrent programs. This book introduces the two most important actor implementations for Scala: the `scala.actors` package of the standard library[2] and the actors package of the Akka project.[3]

Like many powerful concepts, the actor model can be understood and

---

[1]Hewitt *et al.*, "A Universal Modular ACTOR Formalism for Artificial Intelligence" [Hew73]

[2]Haller and Odersky, "Scala Actors: Unifying Thread-based and Event-based Programming" [Hal09]

[3]See http://akka.io/.

used on several levels. On one level, actor-based programming provides an easy way to exchange messages between independently running threads or processes. On another level, actors make concurrent programming generally simpler, because actors let developers focus on high-level concurrency abstractions and shield programmers from intricacies that can easily lead to errors. On an even broader level, actors are about building reliable programs in a world where concurrency is the norm, not the exception—a world that is fast approaching.

This book aims to explain actor-based programming with Scala on all those levels. Before diving into the details of Scala actors, it helps to take a step back and place actors in the context of other approaches to concurrent programming, some of which may already be familiar to you.

1.1   A shift toward parallel hardware

The mainstream computing architectures of the past few decades focused on executing a single thread of sequential instructions faster. That led to an application of Moore's Law to computing performance: processor performance per unit cost has doubled roughly every eighteen months for the last twenty years, and developers counted on that trend to ensure that their increasingly complex programs performed well.[4]

Moore's Law has been remarkably accurate in predicting processor performance, and it is reasonable to expect processor computing capacity to double every one-and-a-half years for at least another decade. To make that increase practical, however, chip designers had to implement a major shift in their design focus in recent years. Instead of trying to improve the clock cycles dedicated to executing a single thread of instructions, new processor designs let you execute many concurrent instruction threads on a single chip. While the clock speed of each computing core on a chip is expected to improve only marginally over the next few years, processors with dozens of cores are already showing up in commodity servers, and multicore chips are the norm even in inexpensive desktops and notebooks.

This shift in the design of high-volume, commodity processor architectures, such as the Intel x86, has at least two ramifications for developers. First, because individual core clock cycles will increase only modestly, we will need to pay renewed attention to the algorithmic efficiency of sequential

---

[4]Sutter, "The Free Lunch Is Over: A Fundamental Turn Toward Concurrency" [Sut05]

code. Second, and more important in the context of actors, we will need to design programs that take maximum advantage of available processor cores. In other words, we not only need to write programs that work correctly on concurrent hardware, but also design programs that opportunistically scale to all available processing units or cores.

1.2   Actors versus threads

In a concurrent program, many independently executing threads, or sequential processes, work together to fulfill an application's requirements. Investigation into concurrent programming has mostly focused on defining how concurrently executing sequential processes can communicate such that a larger process—for example, a program that executed those processes—can proceed predictably.

The two most common ways of communication among concurrent threads are synchronization on shared state and message passing. Many familiar programming constructs, such as semaphores and monitors, are based on shared-state synchronization. Developers of concurrent programs are familiar with those structures. For example, Java programmers can find these structures in the `java.util.concurrent` package in common Java distributions.[5] Among the biggest challenges for anyone using shared-state concurrency are avoiding concurrency hazards, such as data races and deadlocks, and scalability.

Message passing is an alternative way of synchronizing cooperating threads. There are two important categories of systems based on message passing. In channel-based systems, messages are sent to *channels* (or *ports*) that processes can share. Several processes can then receive messages from the same shared channels. Examples of channel-based systems are Message-Passing Interface (MPI)[6] and systems based on the Communicating Sequential Processes (CSP) paradigm,[7] such as the Go language.[8] Systems based on actors (or agents, or Erlang-style processes[9]) are in the second category of

---

[5]Goetz *et al.*, *Java Concurrency in Practice* [Goe06]

[6]Gropp *et al.*, *Using MPI: Portable Parallel Programming with the Message–Passing Interface* [Gro99]

[7]Hoare, "Communicating Sequential Processes" [Hoa78]

[8]See `http://golang.org/`.

[9]Armstrong *et al.*, *Concurrent Programming in Erlang* [Arm95]

message-passing concurrency. In these systems, messages are sent directly to actors; you don't need to create intermediary channels between processes.

An important advantage of message passing over shared-state concurrency is that it makes it easier to avoid *data races*. A data race happens whenever two processes access the same piece of data concurrently and at least one of the accesses is mutating (that is, changing the value of) the data. For example, two Java threads concurrently accessing the same field of the same instance, such that one of the threads reassigns the field, constitutes a data race. If processes communicate only by passing messages, and those messages are immutable, then data races are avoided by design.

Aside from such low-level data races, higher-level data races exist. For example, a process may depend on receiving two messages in a certain order. If it is possible that the two messages are sent concurrently to that process, the program contains a *race condition*; this means that in some runs the program enters an invalid state through concurrent modification of shared state, namely the state of the (shared) receiving process. Leaving data races aside for a moment, anecdotal evidence suggests that message passing in practice also reduces the risk of deadlock.

A potential disadvantage of message passing is that the communication overhead may be high. To communicate, processes have to create and send messages, and these messages are often buffered in queues before they can be received to support asynchronous communication.

By contrast, shared-state concurrency enables direct access to shared memory, as long as it is properly synchronized. To reduce the communication overhead of message passing, large messages should not be transferred by copying the message state; instead, only a reference to the message should be sent. However, this reintroduces the risk for data races when several processes have access to the same mutable (message) data. It is an ongoing research effort to provide static checkers; for instance, the Scala compiler plug-in for uniqueness types[10] that can verify that programs passing mutable messages by reference do not contain data races.

1.3   Scalability

So far, we have compared actors and threads with respect to synchronization (message passing versus shared state) as well as (the avoidance of) concur-

---

[10] Haller and Odersky, "Capabilities for Uniqueness and Borrowing" [Hal10]

rency hazards, such as data races. Another important aspect is *scalability*, that is, the "amount of concurrency" that each paradigm supports well.

Some concurrent systems must scale to an enormous number of concurrent requests. A good example is the real-time ad exchange platform built by Tapad, Inc. for advertising on mobile and connected devices. A real-time ad exchange allows targeting ads to their audience, which is much more effective than buying fixed sets of ad slots to be displayed at random. Supporting ads served by a real-time ad exchange auction on web sites, say, is quite involved: whenever a user opens a page with ads on it, the ad exchange has to obtain information about the current user, it has to forward requests to all registered bidders, and it has to collect the bidders' responses, from which it picks the highest bidder. Finally, the winning bidder's ad is displayed to the user. To guarantee high responsiveness, typically each auction must be carried out in less than 40 milliseconds.

This is where actors come into play. Backed by efficient, event-based execution environments, Scala-based actors (this applies to both Akka and the `scala.actors` package) are much more lightweight than threads on most JVMs, including Oracle's HotSpot JVM. The reason is that threads are typically mapped to heavyweight OS processes to be able to utilize all processor cores available to the JVM. OS processes are heavyweight because their pre-allocated stacks consume a lot of memory, and context switching between them is very expensive on modern processor architectures.[11] As a result, a typical commodity cluster node supports only a few thousand concurrent threads before the JVM runs out of memory. By contrast, the same machine typically supports millions or even tens of millions of concurrent actors.

This enormous scalability provided by Akka's lightweight actors enabled Tapad to achieve their stringent low-latency requirements, scaling their production systems to carry out ad exchange auctions billions of times per month, or tens of thousands of times per second.

1.4 A high-level perspective on concurrency

Let's take a step back and look at actor-based programming from a higher-level perspective. To appreciate the difference, and the relationship, between

---

[11] John L. Hennessy and David A. Patterson, *Computer Architecture: A Quantitative Approach* [Hen11]

more traditional concurrency constructs and actors, it helps to pay a brief visit to the local railroad yard.

Imagine yourself standing on a bridge overlooking the multitude of individual tracks entering the rail yard. You can observe many seemingly independent activities taking place, such as trains arriving and leaving, cars being loaded and unloaded, and so on.

Suppose, then, that your job was to design such a railroad yard. Thinking in terms of threads, locks, monitors, and so on is similar to the problem of figuring out how to make sure that trains running on parallel tracks don't collide. It is an important requirement; without that, the rail yard would be a dangerous place. To accomplish that task, you would employ specialized artifacts, such as semaphores, monitors, and switches.

Actors illuminate the same rail yard from the higher perspective of ensuring that all the concurrent activities taking place at the rail yard progress smoothly: All the delivery vehicles find ways to train cars; all the trains can make their progress through the tracks; and all the activities are properly coordinated.

You will need both perspectives when designing a rail yard: Thinking from the relatively low-level perspective of individual tracks ensures that trains don't inadvertently cross paths; thinking from the perspective of the entire facility helps ensure that your design facilitates smooth overall operation, and that your rail yard can scale, if needed, to accommodate increased traffic. Simply adding new rail tracks only goes so far: you need some overall design principles to ensure that the whole rail yard can grow to handle increased traffic, and that greater traffic can scale up to the full capacity of the tracks.

Working on the relatively low-level details of individual tracks (or problems associated with interleaving threads), on the one hand, and the higher-level perspective of the entire facility (actors) on the other, require somewhat different skills and experience. An actor-based system is often implemented in terms of threads, locks, monitors, and the like, but actors hide those low-level details and allow you to think of concurrent programs from a higher vantage point.

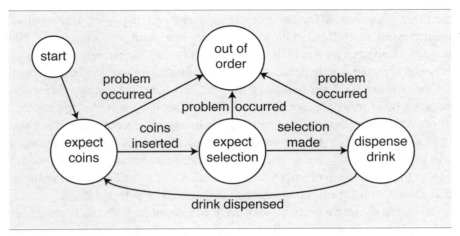

Figure 1.1 · State transitions in a soda machine.

1.5 The indeterministic soda machine

In addition to allowing you to focus on the scalability aspect of concurrent applications, actors' higher-level perspective on concurrency is helpful because it provides a more realistic abstraction for understanding how concurrent applications work. Specifically, concurrent programs exhibit two characteristics that, while also present in sequential applications, are especially pronounced when a program is designed from the ground up to take advantage of concurrency. To see what these are, we need only to stop by the office soda machine.[12]

A soda machine is convenient not only to provide a beverage to quench our thirst, but also because it's a good metaphor for a kind of program that moves from one well-defined state to another. To start out, a soda machine awaits input from the user, perhaps prompting the user to insert coins. Inserting those coins causes the soda machine to enter a state where it can now ask the user to make a selection of the desired drink. As soon as the user makes that selection, the soda machine dispenses a can and moves back into its initial state. On occasion, it may also run out of soda cans—that would place it in an "out of service" state.

At any point in time, a soda machine is aware of only one state. That state is also global to the machine: each component—the coin input device,

---

[12]Hoare, "Communicating Sequential Processes" [Hoa78]

the display unit, the selection entry keypad, the can dispenser, and so on—must consult that global state to determine what action to take next. For instance, if the machine is in the state where the user has already made his or her selection, the can dispenser may release a soda can into the output tray.

In addition to always being in a well-defined state, our simple abstraction suggests two further characteristics of a soda machine: First, that the number of possible states the machine can enter is finite and, second, that given any one of those possible states, we can determine in advance what the next state will be. For instance, if you inserted a sufficient amount of coins, you would expect the machine to prompt you for the choice of drink. And having made that choice, you expect the machine to dispense your selected drink.

Of course, you've probably experienced occasions when soda machines did not behave in such a predictable, deterministic way. You may have inserted plenty of coins, but instead of the machine prompting you for your choice, it delivered an unwelcoming "OUT OF ORDER" message. Or you may not have received any message at all—but also did not receive your frosty refreshment, no matter how hard you pounded the machine. Real-world experience teaches us that soda machines, like most physical objects, are not entirely deterministic. Most of the time they move from one well-defined state to another in an expected, predetermined fashion; but on occasion they move from one state to another—to an error state, for instance—in a way that you could not predict in advance.

A more realistic model of a soda machine, therefore, should include the property of some indeterminism: a model that readily admits a soda machine's ability to shift from one state to another in a way that you could not determine in advance with certainty.

Although we are generally adept at dealing with such indeterminism in physical objects—as well as when dealing with people—when we encounter such indeterminism in software, we tend to consider that behavior a bug. Examining such "bugs" may reveal that they crept into our code because some aspect of our program was not sufficiently specified.

Naturally, as developers, we desire to create programs that are well-specified and, therefore, behave as expected—programs that act exactly in accord with detailed and exhaustive specifications. Indeed, one way to provide more or less exact specifications for code is by writing tests for it.

Concurrent programs, however, are a bit more like soda machines than deterministic sequential code. Concurrent programs, unlike sequential ones, gain many of their benefits because the developer intentionally left some

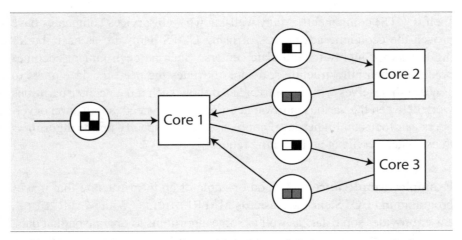

Figure 1.2 · Message passing with indeterministic message ordering.

aspects of a concurrent system unspecified.

The reason for that is easy to understand intuitively when considering a processor with four cores: Suppose that code running on the first core sends messages to code running on the three other cores, and then awaits replies back from each. Upon receiving a reply, the first core performs further processing on the response message.

In practice, the order in which cores 2, 3, and 4 send back their replies is determined by the order in which the three cores finish their computations. If that reply order is left unspecified, then core 1 can start processing a reply as soon as it receives one; it does not have to wait for the slowest core to finish its work.

In this example, leaving the reply order from cores 2, 3, and 4 unspecified helps to best utilize the available computing resources. At the same time, your program can no longer rely on any specific message ordering. Instead, your application must function deterministically even though its component computations, or how those components interact, may not be fully specified.

1.6   Programming the data center

One example of building deterministic systems out of indeterministic component computations are data centers constructed of commercial, off-the-shelf (COTS) components. Many well-known web services companies have proven the economic advantages of using COTS hardware as basic building blocks for highly reliable data centers. Such an environment becomes practical when infrastructure software alleviates the need for developers to concern themselves with the intricacies of how such a data center partitions work between the various hardware components. Instead, application developers can focus on higher-level concerns, such as specifying the algorithms to use when servicing an incoming request.

Example: MapReduce.　A good example of an infrastructure that makes programming COTS clusters easier is MAPREDUCE.[13] With MAPREDUCE, a user provides some data as well as some algorithms to operate on that data, and submits that as a request to the MAPREDUCE infrastructure software. The MAPREDUCE software, in turn, distributes the workload required to compute the specified request across available cluster nodes and returns a result to the user. (In Chapter 9 you will learn how to build an actor-based MAPREDUCE data-processing engine.)

An important aspect of MAPREDUCE is that, upon submitting a job, a user can reasonably expect some result back. For instance, should a node executing parts of a MAPREDUCE job fail to return results within a specified time period, the MAPREDUCE software restarts that component job on another node. Because it guarantees to return a result, MAPREDUCE not only allows an infrastructure to scale a compute-intensive job to a cluster of nodes, but more significantly, MAPREDUCE lends reliability guarantees to the computation. It is that reliability aspect that makes MAPREDUCE suitable for COTS-based compute clusters.

While a developer using MAPREDUCE can expect to receive a result back, exactly when the result will arrive cannot be known prior to submitting the job: the user knows only that a result will be received, but he or she cannot know, in advance, when that will be. More generally, the system provides a guarantee that at some point a computation is brought to completion, but a developer using the system cannot in advance put a time bound on the length of time a computation would run.

Intuitively, it is easy to understand the reason for that: As the infrastructure software partitions the computation, it must communicate with other

---

[13]Dean and Ghemawat, "MapReduce: Simplified Data Processing on Large Clusters" [Dea08]

system components—it must send messages and await replies from individual cluster nodes, for instance. Such communication can incur various latencies, and those communication latencies impact the time it takes to return a result. You can't tell, in advance of submitting a job, how large those latencies will be.

Although some MAPREDUCE implementations aim to ensure that a job returns some (possibly incomplete) results in a specified amount of time, the actors model of concurrent computation is more general: it acknowledges that we may not know in advance just how long a concurrent computation would take. Put another way, you cannot place a time bound in advance on the length a concurrent computation would run. That's in contrast to traditional, sequential algorithms that model computations with well-defined execution times on a given input.

By acknowledging the property of unbounded computational times, actors aim to provide a more realistic model of concurrent computing. While varying communication latencies is easy to grasp in the case of distributed systems or clusters, it is also not possible in a four-core processor to tell in advance how long before cores 2, 3, and 4 will send their replies back to core 1. All we can say is that the replies will eventually arrive.

At the same time, unboundedness does not imply infinite times: While infinity is an intriguing concept, it lends but limited usefulness to realistically modeling computations. The actor model, indeed, requires that a concurrent computation terminate in finite time, but it also acknowledges that it may not be possible to tell, in advance, just how long that time will be.

In the actor model, unboundedness and indeterminism—or, *unbounded indeterminism*—are key attributes of concurrent computing. Although these characteristics are also present in primarily sequential systems, they are pervasive in concurrent programs. Acknowledging these attributes of concurrency and providing a model that allows a developer to reason about concurrent programs in the face of those attributes are the prime goals of actors.

Chapter 2

Messages All the Way Up

Actor-based programming aims to model the complex world of pervasive concurrency with a handful of simple abstractions. Before diving into Scala's actors library, it is helpful to review briefly the most common actor programming constructs. Scala's actors library implements many of these features. At the same time, like many Scala APIs, the actors API is constantly evolving, and future versions will likely provide even more capabilities. In the following birds-eye view of the actor programming model, we refer to features that Scala actors already implement and, when relevant, point out differences between Scala actors and the more general model.

2.1 Control flow and data flow

The designers of the actor programming model started out by defining suitable abstractions for program control flow in concurrent systems. Informally, control flow in a program refers to the choice a program makes about what instructions to execute next. Branching, switch and case statements, as well as making decisions about what to return from a method invocation are all examples of control flow. All but the most trivial programs include some form of control flow.

Developers of sequential programs would not consider control flow a problematic task: After all, we routinely write `if`, `while`, and `for` expressions without thinking too much about the implications of those basic programming constructs. Concurrency, however, can make control flow more difficult to reason about. That's because control flow often depends on some logic, data, or state embedded in the program.

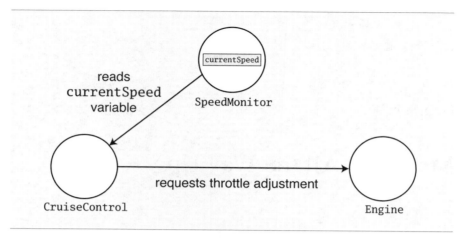

Figure 2.1 · Components holding shared state require synchronization.

In small programs, data and the control structures using that data may be defined close to each other, even in the same object. As a program grows in size, however, control flow decisions will need to consult bits of data—or program state—defined in other parts of the program. For example, the following expression requires access to the currentSpeed and desiredSpeed variables:

```
if (currentSpeed != desiredSpeed)
  changeSpeed(desiredSpeed - currentSpeed)
else
  maintainSpeed()
```

The currentSpeed and desiredSpeed values are defined outside the if-else control structure, perhaps even outside the method or object containing the control flow expression. Similarly, the code implementing the changeSpeed and maintainSpeed methods may access, as well as alter, program state defined elsewhere in the program. Therefore, such methods require access to program state that other objects expose and share. In the previous example, for instance, a SpeedMonitor object may have a public currentSpeed accessor method that any other object in the program can invoke, as illustrated in Figure 2.1. The currentSpeed value then becomes part of the globally visible program state.

Globally visible program state is relatively easy to manage as long as only a single thread is accessing that state at any given point in time. If many concurrently executing threads need to access globally visible state, however, a developer must carefully synchronize access to objects holding that state.[1]

Synchronized access to shared data is not only difficult to get right, but can also reduce the amount of concurrency available in a system.[2] To see why, consider that there are conceptually two different kinds of changes taking place as a concurrent program executes: First, various threads of execution, starting from the beginning of the program, wind their ways through possible paths based on program *control flow*. Those threads, in turn, can alter the values of variables holding the program's state. You can think of those state changes as defining the program's *data flow*. A developer must carefully identify every point in the program's data flow that can be altered by, and in turn affect, other execution threads, and guard against undesired side effects.

Data flow and control flow can interact in subtle ways: For example, in Figure 2.2 data flows from one component to another only if a speed adjustment is needed; otherwise, there is no data flow. While it is not difficult to understand the single interaction illustrated here, understanding such interactions becomes increasingly difficult as the program size and complexity increases.

A proven way to guard against unwanted conflicts between data flow and control flow is to serialize the program's data flow across concurrent threads of execution. Using special serialization constructs, such as locks, monitors, and semaphores, a developer specifies that threads must affect data flow in a strict order.

Defining such serialization in Java or Scala has become much easier with the introduction of the `java.util.concurrent` package. But even with

---

[1] Note that even if global state is not accessed concurrently, care has to be taken to avoid thread visibility issues. For example, on the JVM updating the field of a shared object may not be visible to subsequent threads reading the same field. Only the use of synchronizing operations, such as locking via synchronized methods or accessing volatile fields ensures that updates "happen before" subsequent reads, and therefore become visible. You can find an excellent discussion of thread visibility on the JVM in [Goe06].

[2] One of the reasons why scalability is hard to achieve using locks (or Java-style synchronization) is the fact that coarse-grained locking increases the amount of code that is executed sequentially. Moreover, accessing a small number of locks (or, in the extreme case, a single global lock) from several threads may increase the cost of synchronization significantly.

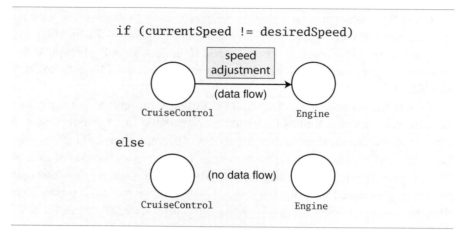

Figure 2.2 · Interaction of data and control flow.

the help of `java.util.concurrent`, writing concurrent programs is still difficult and error prone.

Although serializing access to globally visible program state helps define correct program behavior, it may reduce some of the benefits of concurrent execution. As we mentioned in the previous chapter, the benefits of concurrency come about as a result of having few requirements about the order in which threads wind their way through a program and access program state. In effect, synchronization turns parts of a program into sequential code because only one thread at a time can access the global, or shared, state. Indeed, if control flow through a program relies on globally visible state, there is no way around serialized access to that state without risking incorrect behavior.

A key contribution of the actor model is to define control structures in a way that minimizes reliance on global program state. Instead, all the state—or knowledge—needed to make control flow decisions are encapsulated within the objects that make those decisions. Such objects, in turn, direct control flow only—or mostly—based on data locally visible to them. That *principle of locality,—i.e.,* the notion that control flow decisions are made based on data locally available to the control flow statements only— renders data flow and control flow in a program inseparable, reducing the requirement for synchronization. That, in turn, maximizes the potential for concurrency.

Although actor-based systems consider global state to be evil, in practice some control structures still need access to globally visible state. Recent additions to Scala's actors library make it easier to reason about such shared state in the context of actors, and we will highlight those features in later chapters of this book.

2.2 Actors and messages

The main mechanism for unifying control flow and data flow is a special abstraction, the actor, and the message-based communication that takes place between actors. An actor is any object that can exchange messages with other actors. In the actor programming model, actors communicate solely by passing messages to each other.

In a pure actor system, every object is an actor. For instance, in Erlang, another language that defines an actor programming model, even atomic objects, such as Ints and Strings, are actors. Scala's actors library, by contrast, allows you to easily turn any Scala object into an actor, but does not require that all objects be actors.

Actors have a uniform public interface: An actor can, in general, accept any kind of message. When an actor receives a message from another actor, the receiving actor examines, or *evaluates*, the incoming message. Based on the contents and type of that message, the receiving actor may find the message interesting; otherwise, it simply discards the message. When an actor is interested in an incoming message, it may perform some action in response to that message. The action depends on the actor's internal script or program, as well as the actor's current state. The ability to perform actions in response to incoming messages is what makes an object an actor.

An actor's response to an incoming message can take different forms. The simplest response is to merely evaluate the message's content. Performing addition of integers x and y in an actor-based system, for instance, would consist of a message containing x and y sent to an actor capable of adding the integers together. In that case, the arithmetic actor would simply *evaluate* the sum of x and y.

Of course, merely adding two numbers together is of little use if the result is not visible outside the actor performing the evaluation. Thus, a more useful actor message would contain the address of another actor interested in receiving the result. This is illustrated in Figure 2.3.

A reference to another actor in a message is the receiving actor's *continu-*

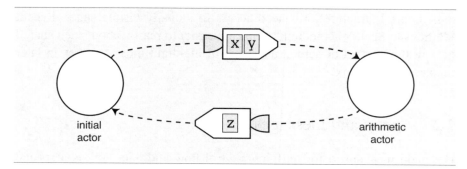

Figure 2.3 · The simplest actor computation: adding x and y together.

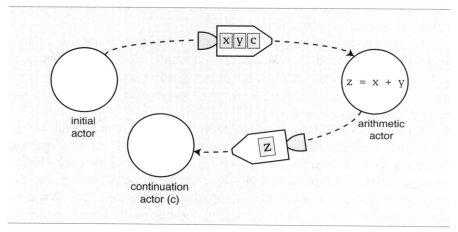

Figure 2.4 · Actor computation with continuation message passing.

ation. Upon evaluating a message according to an internal script, an actor can send the results of that evaluation to its continuation. Including references to a continuation in an actor's message means that the actor programming model implicitly supports the *continuation-passing style* (CPS), but generalized to concurrent programming.[3] This is illustrated in Figure 2.4.

The simplest kind of continuation is a reference to the sending actor. Having access to a message's sender is so convenient that the Scala actors library implicitly includes a reference to the sending actor in messages, as shown in Figure 2.5.

---

[3] Agha, "Concurrent Object-Oriented Programming" [Agh90]

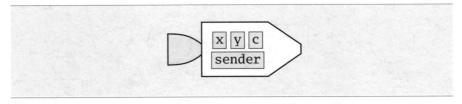

Figure 2.5 · Every message carries a sender reference.

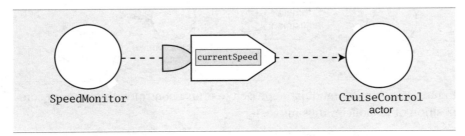

Figure 2.6 · CruiseControl actor receiving currentSpeed message.

An actor's continuation is a key element of control flow in actor-based programming. Program control flows from one actor to another as continuations are passed between actors. At the same time, the actor message that sends possible continuations may also include the data required by the actor to determine control flow. The actor model unifies control flow and data flow in the sense that data as well as an actor's continuation can be passed inside the same message.

That unified view makes it easier to design actor-based programs. When designing a program with actors, it is helpful to first determine the kinds of control flow your code requires. Those control decisions would be made by actors. Thus, you would next define what data those control flow decisions require, and send that data inside messages to the appropriate actors.

The speed maintenance control structure in the previous example, for instance, requires a decision about whether to maintain or change the current speed. That decision needs just the current and desired speed values. The simplest implementation merely evaluates the values supplied by incoming messages and takes appropriate action based on those values, as illustrated in Figure 2.6. Note that the message sender does not have to be an actor.

A more modular approach would define an actor responsible for deciding

21

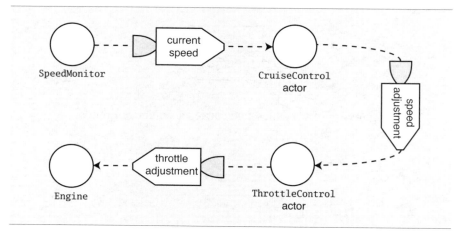

Figure 2.7 · A more modular approach to cruise control with further decomposition of responsibilities into actors.

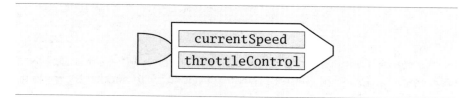

Figure 2.8 · A throttleControl continuation included in a message.

the required speed adjustment, and would then send the result to a continuation, as shown in Figure 2.7.

One advantage of the actor-based approach is that it allows the continuation of CruiseControl—ThrottleControl—to be defined sometime after CruiseControl is defined—and even after an instance of CruiseControl is already initialized and loaded into memory: ThrottleControl is simply an actor with the uniform actor interface to receive messages. Thus all CruiseControl needs is a reference to the continuation actor, such as that actor's address.

The ability to perform such extreme *late binding* of a continuation allows developers to incrementally add knowledge—such as control flow—to an actor-based system. Indeed, actors grew out of the desire to create large knowledge-based systems in an incremental fashion. A continuation actor included in a message, such as the `throttleControl` continuation shown in Figure 2.8, affects control flow and accommodates late binding in an actor system.

Late binding in actor control flow is also an important tool in lending robustness to an actor-based system. For instance, an actor may be redundantly defined, allowing a message sender to send replicated messages.

If actors interacting via messages sounds similar to how objects communicate in an object-oriented system, that likeness is no mere coincidence. Indeed, the actor model was developed at the same time the first object-oriented languages were designed, and was, in turn, influenced by object-oriented concepts. Alan Kay, an inventor of object-oriented programming, noted that message passing between objects is more central to object-oriented programming than objects themselves are. In an email on messaging to a Smalltalk discussion group, Kay wrote:[4]

> The big idea is "messaging" – that is what the kernel of Smalltalk/ Squeak is all about (and it's something that was never quite completed in our Xerox PARC phase). The Japanese have a small word – ma – for "that which is in between" – perhaps the nearest English equivalent is "interstitial." The key in making great and growable systems is much more to design how its modules communicate rather than what their internal properties and behaviors should be...

You can view the actor model as a special case of object-oriented programming where all communication between objects takes place via message passing, and when an object's internal state changes only in response to messages.

2.3   Actor creation

An actor can send a message only to its acquaintances—other actors whose addresses it knows. Continuation passing is one way in which an actor can learn the addresses of other actors. Another way is for an actor to create other actors as part of its evaluation of a message. Such newly created actors— *child actors*—can have an independent lifetime from that of the creating ac-

---

[4]Kay, an email on messaging in Smalltalk/Squeak. [Kay98]

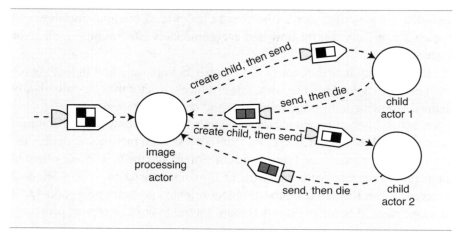

Figure 2.9 · Creating and delegating work to child actors.

tor. Having created new actors, the creating actor can send messages to the new actors, possibly passing its own address as part of those messages.

An actor's ability to create other actors makes it easy to implement fork-join parallelism. For instance, upon receiving a message, an actor may decide to divide up a potentially compute-intensive job and create child actors for the purpose of processing parts of that larger computation. As illustrated in Figure 2.9, a creator actor would divvy up work among its child actors, and wait for the children to complete their work and send their results back to the parent. Once all the results have been collected, the parent actor can summarize those results, possibly sending the results to yet another actor, or continuation. We will provide several examples of fork-join parallelism in later chapters.

2.4 Actor events

Although we have so far focused on an actor's ability to send messages to other actors, all the "action" in an actor takes place at the time a message is *received*. Receiving messages and creating other actors are two examples of events in an actor system.

Events and their relationships illuminate how physical phenomena inspired the actor programming model. For instance, when actor B receives a

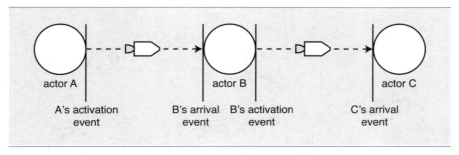

Figure 2.10 · B's arrival event activates C's arrival event.

message from actor A, B can send a message to C as a result, defining an order of *arrival events*. In this example, which is illustrated in Figure 2.10, the message sent to B caused, or *activated*, C's arrival event.

In their seminal paper on the "Laws for Communicating Parallel Processes,"[5] Carl Hewitt and Henry Baker noted that:

> Activation is the actor notion of causality... A crude analogy from physics may make activation more clear. A photon (message) is received by an atom (target), which puts it into an excited state. After a while, the atom gives off one or more photons and returns to its ground state. These emitted photons may be received by other atoms, and these secondary events are said to be activated by the first event.

In addition to arrival events and actor creation events, an actor-based system also includes some "initial event" that gets the ball rolling, so to speak. Causality extends to all three types of events: The initial event must precede all other events and may include a set of initial actors. Those actors can process activation events from each other in any order. Finally, and obviously, an actor's creation event must always precede activation events targeting that actor.

Figure 2.11 shows that arrival and activation events nicely line up in a time-ordered sequence, one event always occurring before the other. Indeed, we can describe an actor-based computation as a linear ordering of combined arrival and activation events: A computation starts with some event, which

---

[5]Hewitt and Baker, "Laws for Communicating Parallel Processes" [HB77]

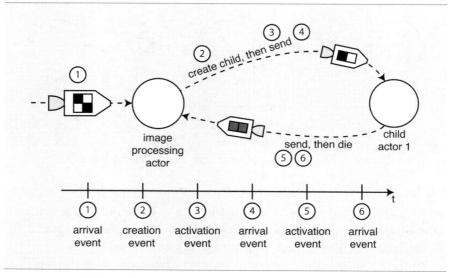

Figure 2.11 · Event causality in an actor system.

is then followed by a finite number of other events, and is finally terminated by the computation's last event. The order of events is strict in the sense that an event can only be influenced by other events that preceded it.

When we say one event occurs before—or after—another event, we intuitively refer to some notion of time. In a sequential computation, when the entire program state is shared globally, the sequence of events that makes up the computation refers to the global time: time shared by all objects participating in the computation. An actor-based system, by contrast, splits the global program state into many local states held by each actor. Those actors interact merely by passing messages, and have no reference to a shared notion of time. Instead, arrival orderings of events in an actor-based system refer to the time *local* to an actor—there is no requirement to have a notion of global time.

Viewing computations as a partial order of actor events occurring in local time to an actor turns out to be a powerful abstraction. The designers of the actor programming model demonstrated that you can implement any control structure as a sequence of actor events. Because actor-based programming is designed with concurrency assumed, it is theoretically possible to implement any sequential program in a concurrent manner with actor messaging.

2.5   Asynchronous communication

The reason actors ignore message sending as an event, and emphasize message arrival instead, is that message transmission between actors may incur some delay. For instance, actor A may send a message to B, and include C as a continuation. Although A activates C's message, there may be some delay between A sending the message and C receiving a message. The delay may be due to some processing time incurred at B as well as to communication latency. Considering message delay as an integral part of a computation is another way actor communication differs from simple object invocation in object-oriented programming.

Practical actor-based systems deal with message delay by offering the ability to asynchronously pass messages between actors. Once an actor dispatches a message to another actor, the sending actor can resume its work immediately. The sending actor does not need to wait for a reply. Indeed, some actor messages will never produce a reply. When replies are expected, those will also be sent asynchronously. As Carl Hewitt noted, actors communicate via messages following the principle of "send it and forget it."

You might already be familiar with the concept of asynchronous message passing from modern web programming models, such as AJAX.[6] AJAX is based on asynchronous messages exchanged between a web browser and a remote server. AJAX has proven practical in web applications because an unknown amount of latency may be incurred both in the network communication as well as in the server processing an incoming message. A web client can simply send a message to the server, register a listener for future replies from the server, and immediately return control to the user interface, keeping the application responsive to user interaction.

Similarly, asynchronous messages in actor communication means that the actor model works equally well across networks as it does in a single address space. Indeed, the Scala actors library defines both "local" as well as "remote" actors. Switching between local and remote actors is surprisingly simple, because asynchronous messaging works well in either case. In addition to asynchronous messaging primitives, the Scala actors API provides for synchronous message sending as well.

The "send it and forget it" principle assumes that all messages sent are eventually received by the target actor. Although in many systems the no-

---

[6]AJAX was originally coined as an acronym for Asynchronous JavaScript and XML.

tion of "lost" messages is real—for instance, the server hosting a target actor may crash resulting in the target never receiving the message—the actor model assumes that infrastructure components ensure reliable message transmission. In other words, the actor model assumes a finite—although initially unknown or *unbounded*—amount of time between message sending and message transmission.

How to achieve reliable message transmission is no more a part of the actor-based programming model than, say, the problem of high availability for database management systems is a part of relational algebra and SQL programming. The actor programming model nevertheless makes the implementation of highly reliable and available systems much easier: reliability is often achieved through redundancy and replication, and actors' natural propensity to work well in distributed, concurrent systems serves those needs well. We will provide examples and best practices for achieving reliable actor communication throughout this book.

2.6   You've got mail: indeterminacy and the role of the arbiter

Although the actor model doesn't prescribe a mechanism for reliable message delivery, it acknowledges that many messages may be sent to a single actor in quick succession. Rapidly arriving messages could result in a sort of denial-of-service for the actor, rendering the actor incapable of processing the incoming message flow. To alleviate that problem, the actor model requires that a special object be provided by each actor for the purpose of receiving messages and holding those messages until the actor is able to process them. Such an arbiter is often called a *mailbox*, since it provides a function similar to, say, an email account: messages can arrive in the mailbox at any time and will be held there until the recipient is ready to process them.

Email clients give you complete freedom in choosing the order in which you read new messages. In a similar way, an actor's mailbox may provide the actor with messages in any order. The only requirement is that an actor process one message at a time from its mailbox. Because you cannot determine in advance the order in which an actor processes messages—the order of message delivery is *indeterminate*—you must ensure that the correctness of an actor-based program does not depend on any specific message order.[7]

The actor model makes such programming practices easy, however, because any sort of data can be contained in an actor message, and also because an actor is able to maintain its own state. Consider, for instance, an actor that sums up two integers and sends the result to a third actor. In the simplest implementation, a single actor message would contain the two integers as well as the continuation where the sum would be sent to.

A different implementation may process integers from separate senders. That implementation would expect a message with a single integer, in addition to a name that uniquely identifies the addition calculation. Since addition is commutative, the order of message transmission does not matter: The addition actor saves away the initial value received via the first actor message. Upon receiving the second integer with a similarly named calculation, the addition actor performs the arithmetic operation and sends the reply.

Consider, however, a version of the arithmetic actor designed to add a set of integers. One problematic approach would be to have each integer message include a `lastElement` flag indicating whether it is the terminal element of the series. As soon as the actor receives the last element in the series, it could send the result to the continuation. But since we cannot guarantee the message delivery order, the last element may be received in any order, resulting in possibly the premature sending of the result.

You can often alleviate reliance on message ordering by refactoring the actor communication, *i.e.*, reworking the messages' contents. For instance, the message described previously could include the number of elements in the series, instead of the `lastElement` flag. Throughout this book, we will include tips and techniques to design actor communication that does not rely on message order.

Indeterminacy in the actor model results because an actor's mailbox, or *arbiter*, can receive and provide messages to the actor in any order. You can't guarantee or even specify the order of message arrival due to the inevitable latencies in message transmission between actors: while a message is guaranteed to eventually arrive, the message's transmission time is unbounded.

As we mentioned in the previous chapter, a programming model based on unbounded indeterminism powerfully captures the nature of concurrent

---

[7] In Scala actors, the guarantees of message delivery are a bit stronger than the full indeterminacy of the pure actor programming model. If an actor sends several messages to the same receiver, those messages arrive in the receiving actor's in the order in which they have been sent.

computation. In the actor model, concurrency is the norm, while sequential computation is a special case.

2.7   Actor life cycle

Because of their readiness to process incoming messages, actors can be imagined as "live objects," or objects with a life cycle. Unlike the lives of movie actors, the life of an actor object is rather boring: Once an actor is created, it typically starts processing incoming messages. Once an actor has exceeded its useful life, it can be stopped and destroyed, either of its own accord, or as a result of some "poison pill" message.

Creating and starting an actor are separate, although closely related, tasks. In Scala, actors are plain old Scala objects, and can therefore be created via their constructors. An actor starts processing incoming messages after it has been started, which is similar to starting a Java thread.

In practice, it is useful for actors to be able to monitor each others' life-cycle events. In the fork-join example, for instance, a child actor may decide to terminate upon sending its response to the parent, in order to free up memory. At that point, it could send a message to its parent actor indicating its exit. In Scala Actors, life-cycle monitoring is supported through actor *links*. Actor linking is explained in detail in Section 6.2.

Chapter 3

Scala's Language Support for Actors

The Scala Actors API defines a domain-specific language, hosted inside Scala, that appears to the programmer as if Scala has language-level support for actors. Scala has proven to be an especially hospitable environment for actors, in part, because of several language features that allow you to create DSL-like APIs. Scala also defines language features that, in turn, make it friendly to concurrent programming.

This chapter reviews the Scala features most relevant to actors for the Java developer who has little or no experience with Scala. If you are already familiar with Scala features such as passing functions into methods, by-name parameters, partially applied functions, and pattern matching, you can safely skip this chapter.

3.1   A scalable language

Systems languages, such as C, C++, and to some extent Java, have long been the part and parcel of developing complex, large-scale software, often with critical performance requirements. By contrast, scripting languages have filled the need of one-off programming tasks and of tying together components developed in more complex and performant languages, often performed as a batch job. Because they filled different niches, systems languages and their associated libraries evolved to become relatively more complex compared to their scripting-language cousins.

Instead of having to choose between a simpler but less-performant scripting language, on the one hand, and a speedy but complex systems language, on the other, Scala designer Martin Odersky envisioned a language that would be suitable for (or *scale to*) large and complex systems as well as small scripting tasks.

In almost every development team, some developers are more skilled in a language while some have more experience with a problem domain. Scala aims to present complexity at the level most appropriate for a developer. Developers more skilled in the language itself are able to define new, relatively simple language constructs that address the needs of domain experts who may have less Scala experience.

Scala's division-of-labor aspect has been applied to software testing, data analysis, as well as to the area of concurrency and actor programming. The Actor API developers defined a handful of programming constructs that present a simple and straightforward way to work with actors, without the API user having to understand the intricacies of actor concurrency. In essence, the Scala Actor API "grows" the Scala language into a robust, concurrent programming environment.

Another way in which Scala achieves scalability is via its reliance on the Java runtime environment. Scala code compiles to Java bytecode. As a result, Scala is fully binary-compatible with Java, although it is not source-code compatible. Scala's developers invested much effort to ensure that the compiled bytecode is nearly as efficient as if the code were compiled from Java language sources.

A benefit of Scala being a JVM language is that Scala code can use any existing Java library. Invoking a Java method from Scala is just like invoking that method from another Java class. That seamless binary compatibility also assists the novice Scala developer to ease into Scala one step at a time. Indeed, a good way to get started with Scala is to implement a piece of new functionality in Scala in the context of an existing Java project. The current leading Scala IDEs, such as Eclipse and IntelliJ, support mixed Java and Scala projects.

Although you don't need to understand the full implementation details of the Actor API to start developing concurrent programs in Scala, you will need to grasp a handful of Scala language features in order to follow the examples in the next chapters.

3.2   Immutable and mutable state

Scala code can look quite familiar to a Java developer, but Scala is typically more concise than Java. Indeed, many Scala features are designed to make code cleaner and easier to read, all the way from small syntactic details to control structures and program organization.

For instance, the Scala compiler attempts to infer variable types, saving you some finger typing:

```
val fred = "Fred"
val customerOrder = new CustomerOrder
val count = 10
```

In the above examples, the compiler will properly infer the type of each variable. However, you can also explicitly specify a variable's type:

```
val count: Int = 10
```

The `vals` in the previous examples declare immutable variables, analogous to what Java's `final` keyword accomplishes: an immutable variable cannot be re-assigned after its initial declaration. You will note a preference for immutable variables and, by extension, immutable object state, in Scala code. Favoring immutable data structures is another way Scala supports development practices that scale from short scripts to large applications, and from single-threaded programs to highly concurrent ones. Since concurrent code allows access to object state from possibly many threads, immutable objects better lend themselves to scaling via concurrency. If you wish, however, you can declare a mutable variable via the `var` keyword.

3.3   Methods and classes

Scala methods start with the `def` keyword, and do not require the `return` keyword. Instead, the value of the last expression in the method is returned. The compiler can also infer the method's return type:

```
def addOne(x: Int) = { x + 1 }
```

33

Methods that consist of a single expression can alternatively leave out the surrounding braces:

```scala
def addOne(x: Int) = x + 1
```

As in Java, Scala methods are part of a class:

```scala
class Calculator {
  def addOne(x: Int) = x + 1
}
```

Scala inheritance works in conjunction with existing Java code, too. For instance, you can implement an HttpServlet in Scala by extending it, as shown in Listing 3.1. As the example illustrates, Scala has no checked exceptions.

```scala
import javax.servlet.http._ // _ means a wildcard
class ScalaServlet extends HttpServlet {
  override def init() {
    super.init.()
    // Do something
  }
  override def doGet(req: HttpServletRequest,
      res: HttpServletResponse) { // No checked exceptions
    // Handle the get() method
  }
}
```

Listing 3.1 · Extending HttpServlet from Scala

3.4 First-class functions

Scala also supports functions that are not declared to be part of a specific class. Indeed, functions in Scala are first-class objects: you can do anything with a function that you can do with an object value, such as assign a function to a variable, pass a function as a parameter to another function, or return a function from another function.

Because function values are such an important aspect of Scala programs, the language provides a convenient way to define function values via function literals. Function literals have no names, and can be used like any other type of value.

The Scala APIs are rich in methods that consume function values. For instance, Scala's `List` class defines a method, `map`, that consumes a function, applies the function to all list elements, and returns a new list of the resulting values. Using a function literal to define the parameter passed into map affords a concise way to transform list elements:

```scala
val myList = List(1, 2, 3)
val plusOne = myList.map(x => x + 1)
...
List(2, 3, 4)
```

There's an even handier way to define the above function literal:

```scala
val plusTwo = myList.map(_ + 2)
...
List(3, 4, 5)
```

The underscore (_) in this function literal stands for the argument being passed to the function.

By-name parameters

In Java, all method parameters are passed by value, even object references: the parameter value is evaluated before invoking the method. Scala's default behavior also passes parameters by value. However, when passing a function or a function literal to a method, it is sometimes helpful to delay the evaluation of the parameter value:

```scala
// Pseudocode
myMethod(someBlockOfCodeOrFunction) = {
```

35

```
  // Do something else first
  ...
  // Evaluate the parameter and return its value
  someBlockOfCodeOrFunction()
}
```

Scala supports that behavior with by-name parameters. By-name parameters are not evaluated when the method is invoked; instead, you can delay the parameter's evaluation to the first time you refer to that parameter *by name* inside the method. To pass a parameter by name, prefix the parameter type with =>, as shown here:

```
def doItByName(block: => Any) {
  println("Doing something first")
  block
}
```

Invoking the doItByName method, you would get the following output:

```
doItByName(println("Hello, there"))
...
Doing something first
Hello, there
```

3.5   Functions as control structures

Java developers seldom think about control structures such as for, while, or if—these are part of the Java language. Scala, by contrast, has a richer set of control structures, and many of those control structures are implemented as methods that consume functions as their parameters. The Actor API defines a handful of carefully crafted control structures designed to direct actor behavior, such as act, receive, or reply.

Scala makes creating new control structures even more natural with a little syntactic sugar: when a Scala method has only one parameter, you can surround the method argument with curly braces instead of parentheses. The following are equivalent uses of the same method:

```
doItByName(println("Hello, there"))
doItByName {
  println("Hello, there")
}
```

That syntax can make an API more natural to use. Consider the common pattern of using a resource, such as a network connection: you first open or otherwise acquire the resource, use the resource, and finally close or relinquish the resource. That pattern is sometimes referred to as the loan pattern, since the resource is effectively "loaned" to the code making use of the resource.

The following code illustrates the use of the loan pattern in a context that you might be familiar with, a Java Persistence Architecture (JPA) transaction. JPA requires that you access persistent data inside a JPA transaction. In an environment where you manage your transaction demarcation, you must take care to start a transaction, access the persistent data, and then close the transaction.

A developer familiar with JPA can define a control abstraction, txn, that encapsulates that desired behavior. Other developers, perhaps less persnickety when it comes to resource allocation, can use this control structure without having to worry about starting and closing transactions.

From a user's perspective, the control structure looks as follows:

```
class InventoryManager {
  def currentInventory() = {
    txn {
      entityManager.createQuery(
        "select bk from Book bk"
      ).getResultList()
    }
  }
}
```

In this example, txn is a method that takes a block of code, or a function, as an argument. Because the method has a single argument, the parameter can be surrounded with curly braces.

37

The more JPA-savvy developer implementing txn would open the transaction, make entityManager available to the function passed in as the argument, and close the transaction, handling any errors along the way. The following is one implementation, using a by-name parameter:

```
def txn[T](block: => T): T = {
  val entityMan = getEntityManager()  // Obtain the JPA entity manager
                                      // Code is not shown
  EmThreadLocal.set(entityMan)        // Set the entity manager in a
                                      // threadlocal variable so that the
                                      // entity manager is available to
                                      // code performed under the transaction
  val tx = entityMan.getTransaction()
  try {
    tx.begin()
    val result = block                // Execute the code passed into txn
    tx.commit()
    res                               // Return the results, if any
  }
  finally {
    if (entityMan.geTransaction().isActive())
      entityMan.getTransaction().rollback()
    if (entityMan.isOpen())
      entityMan.close()
    EmTheadLocal.remove()
  }
}
```

Listing 3.2 · Implementation of the txn control structure

The code snippet shown in Listing 3.2 provides an example of Scala's type parameters. The txn[T](block: => T): T in the method declaration roughly says: txn takes a block that, once executed, returns a value having type T, and then the entire txn method returns this T value. Thus, the txn method's return type is T.

The [T] portion of the method declaration declares a type parameter for T. Type parameters allow the compiler to check the type-safety of your code: If block passed into the method returns, say, a java.util.List of

Book objects, then T will refer to that type, and the compiler ensures txn also returns a Book list. If you tried to return some other type from txn, the program would not compile.

As this example illustrates, defining a new control structure is typically a more complex task than using that control structure from client code: the client developer, for instance, did not have to worry about starting and committing a transaction, or even about type parameters. The new control structure allows the client code to remain concise but still robust. That division of complexity allows members of a development team to focus on what they know best.

The Scala Actor API follows that division-of-labor tenet: the Actor API abstracts away much of the tedium of message sending and handling behind the facade of several simple control structures. You can compose complex actor programs by combining those control structures into the exact message sending and processing behaviors you desire.

Currying

The syntactic sugar of using curly braces instead of parentheses to surround method parameters—a feature that comes in handy when defining new control structures—works only for methods that have a single argument; it won't work for methods whose parameter lists consist of more than one element.

Scala allows you to transform a method with several parameters to an equivalent chain of back-to-back methods, each with a single argument. The following methods produce identical results:

```
def add(x: Int, y: Int) = x + y
...
add(3, 5)
8
def curriedAdd(x: Int)(y: Int) = x + x
...
add(3)(5)
8
```

The compiler translates the second method definition into two method invocations. The first method consumes the initial argument, x, and results in a second function. That second function now consumes y, and returns the sum of x and y:

```
def first(x: Int) = { (y: Int) => x + y }
val second = first(3)
...
second(5)
8
```

Curried functions are useful when you wish to create a control structure with two or more arguments. Consider, for instance, the case of a control structure that closes a network socket after the socket is used. Here, you would want to pass the socket as one argument to the control structure, and the function that uses the socket, as the other. You can specify this by presenting two lists of arguments to the control structure, each argument list consisting of just a single element. To make the code easier to read, the second argument is specified between curly braces:

```
val socket: Socket

withSocket(socket) {
  s => // Read from the socket, socket is available as s
}       // Socket is closed
```

You could implement the withSocket control structure as follows:

```
def withSocket[T](socket: Socket)(f: Socket => T): T = {
  try {
    f(socket)
  }
  finally {
    socket.close()
  }
}
```

Structural typing

Scala offers another language feature that can make a control structure, such as withSocket, more general. The Socket class is not alone in having a close() method: files, network connections, database connections, and so forth must be closed after use, and therefore define a close() method. These classes do not share a common supertype; having a close method is the only commonality between these classes. It would be ideal to generalize withSocket to operate on any class with a close method.

Structural typing allows us to specify a type based not on a shared supertype, but on a structural commonality, such as having a close() method:

```
def withResource[A <: {def close(): Unit}, B]
    (param: A) (f: A => B): B = {
  try {
    f(param)
  }
  finally {
    param.close()
  }
}
```

The withResource method declares a type parameter A, which is "at least" a type with a close() method that returns a Unit, Scala's equivalent of void. The <: symbol indicates an upper type bound: A must be a subtype of the type referred to on the right of the <: symbol, in this case, a type that structurally conforms to the code block with the close() method.

Thus, the first value parameter of withResource() must be a subtype of anything with a close() method—for instance, a Socket—and the second value parameter is a function that consumes this instance and returns a value of a different type, B.

3.6 Pattern matching and case classes

One of the core tenets of object-oriented programming is encapsulation: objects have private state, and access to that private state is controlled by methods on the object. Encapsulation encourages scalable design in that an object's implementation can evolve without impacting client code. While encapsulation is simple to achieve with pure value-objects, where getter and setter methods may suffice, more complex objects can contain state for which there are no readily available accessor methods.

41

Pattern matching, a functional language technique that dates back to the 1970s, helps in those situations. Similar to a `switch` statement, pattern matching allows you to match an object's state against a pattern. That pattern closely mirrors the code used to create the object.

For instance, consider a `ConfirmationMessage`, with a `paymentStatus` and a `shippingStatus` field. Pattern matching allows you to use the object's state in `switch`-like manner:

```
val status =
  message match {
    case ConfirmationMessage(Paid, Shipped) =>
      Status("Order on its way")
    case ConfirmationMessage(Paid, Pending) =>
      Status("Wrapping the order")
    case ConfirmationMessage(Paid, Returned) =>
      Status("That's too bad!")
    case ConfirmationMessage(Declined, _) =>
      Status("Wrong credit card")
    case _ => Status("Unknown status")
  }
```

Although `ConfirmationMessage(Paid, Shipped)` looks like the construction of a `ConfirmationMessage` instance, it instead denotes a pattern against which `message` is matched. Scala's pattern matching picks apart the `message` object and finds out if `message` is a `ConfirmationMessage` type, and if so, whether it's `paymentStatus` and `shippingStatus` values are `Paid` and `Shipped`, respectively.

The first pattern matching `message` causes the expression on the right of => to evaluate; subsequent patterns are not matched. If the expression to the right returns a value, as in this example, the value of that expression is returned from the `match`.

As the example illustrates, you can use wildcards in several places: the underscore in `ConfirmationMessage(Declined, _)` means that we don't care about the shipping status value. And, in the last line of the `match` block, a wildcard ensures that an unknown message status is matched.

The actor API uses pattern matching extensively in incoming message processing. An actor's message typically carries one or more value objects. For instance, a `ConfirmationMessage` includes references to values paymentStatus and shippingStatus. ConfirmationMessage's purpose, then, is to bundle those constituent values.

Scala's case classes provide a convenient way to define classes whose constructor wraps other data elements that are part of the class:

```
case class ConfirmationMessage(
  paymentStatus: String,
  shippingStatus: String
)
```

All you need to do is preface the class with case, and list the class's constituent objects in the constructors. The Scala compiler adds some syntactic sugar to such classes, such as a proper implementation of equals and hashCode, and makes it possible for you to use case classes in pattern matching. You would almost always want to define your actor messages as Scala case classes.

Note that in the current implementation of Scala, match is a language construct, not a method, even though match appears as a control structure, similar to the control structures we defined earlier with methods. Indeed, in earlier versions of Scala, match was implemented as a method, but various implementation issues led to it now being defined as a special keyword. Nevertheless, for all practical purposes, you can think of match as a method consuming a list of pattern matching cases as its argument.

In the above example, the last pattern matching case, an underscore (_), is a wildcard that matches anything. But what if you left out that wild-card pattern? With the above example, the Scala compiler would complain and, if you ever passed into it a ConfirmationMessage that does not match one of your cases, match would result in a runtime exception.

Without a wild-card case pattern, the pattern matching cases match only a subset of possible argument values to match. Since a Scala function is an object of a specific type (a function type), you can create a function subclass that defines the function for only a specific range of the function's arguments. For instance, without the last wild-card pattern, the above definition of match defines the function for only four argument values (actually, the wildcard in the third case may match additional values, too). Scala's pattern matching is implemented in terms of such partial functions; and you will see the PartialFunction class as an argument type in the actor API.

Chapter 4

Actor Chat

The previous chapters illustrate the actor programming model's focus on message passing. Not surprisingly, much of Scala's actors library defines a rich set of programming constructs for sending and receiving messages. These constructs appear as an internal domain-specific language (DSL) to the developer. This chapter illustrates the key elements of Scala's actor DSL with a quintessential messaging application: a chat program.

A chat program allows users to communicate with each other by exchanging messages about various topics. Each topic is represented by a chat room. Users interested in following a discussion about a topic can subscribe to a chat room. Once subscribed, a user may send messages to the chat room and, in turn, receive messages from other chat room subscribers. The chat room maintains a session of subscribers. Figure 4.1 provides an overview of the chat application developed in this chapter.

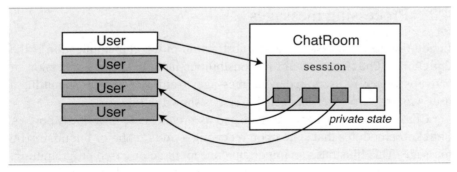

Figure 4.1 · An actor chat application.

4.1   Defining message classes

The chat room application's communication centers around messages: a user sends a Subscribe message to indicate a desire to send and receive chat room messages, an Unsubscribe message to remove him or herself from the chat room's session, and a UserPost message to forward to the chat room's subscribers. When a chat room receives a user's UserPost message, it forwards that message's contents to each of its subscribers inside a Post message. The chat room also makes sure not to send a message back to the user posting that message, lest an unfriendly "echo" effect appear.

A typical first step in developing an actor-based program is to define the message classes that represent the application's communication pattern. Scala's case classes come in handy for defining actor messages. As you'll see shortly, case classes are especially useful in the context of pattern matching, a key technique in actor message processing. Listing 4.1 shows how to define the message classes for our chat application.

```scala
case class User(name: String)
case class Subscribe(user: User)
case class Unsubscribe(user: User)
case class Post(msg: String)
case class UserPost(user: User, post: Post)
```

Listing 4.1 · Case classes for Users and messages.

4.2   Processing messages

In addition to the messages, a key abstraction in the chat application is the ChatRoom. ChatRoom's main responsibilities include keeping a session of actively logged-in users, receiving messages from users, and transmitting a user's message to other interested users, as shown in Figure 4.2.

Chat room subscribers are managed as private state of a ChatRoom. A ChatRoom modifies that state upon receiving a Subscribe or Unsubscribe message. This illustrates an important concept of actor-based programming: some messages sent to an actor alter the actor's internal state and that, in turn, affects the actor's subsequent behavior. For instance, a new Subscribe

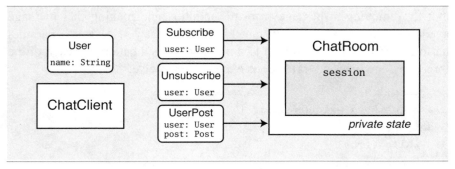

Figure 4.2 · Message communication between chat room and users.

message causes a ChatRoom to forward subsequent Post messages to the newly registered user, affecting the application's message flow.

ChatRoom's message-handling responsibilities are implemented by extending the scala.actors.Actor trait. Extending the Actor trait means that a ChatRoom benefits from the Actor trait's message handling infrastructure, such as the mailbox.

All message handling in an actor takes place inside the act method; Listing 4.2 shows how to define it.

```scala
import scala.actors.Actor

class ChatRoom extends Actor {
  def act() {
    // the actor's behavior
  }
}
```

Listing 4.2 · Defining act.

Message processing inside the act method starts when you invoke start on the actor:

```scala
val chatRoom = new ChatRoom
chatRoom.start()
```

A key task in actor-message processing is to obtain the next available message from the actor's mailbox. Actor's receive method accomplishes

47

that by removing a message from the mailbox and making that message available to a series of pattern matching cases that you pass as a parameter to `receive`. The example in Listing 4.3 defines a pattern for each of the three message types a ChatRoom is expected to receive.

```scala
class ChatRoom extends Actor {
  def act() {
    while (true) {
      receive {
        case Subscribe(user) =>      // handle subscriptions
        case Unsubscribe(user) =>    // handle unsubscriptions
        case UserPost(user, post) => // handle user posts
      }
    }
  }
}
```

Listing 4.3 · Incoming message patterns.

Each invocation of `receive` obtains the next available message from the actor's mailbox, and passes that message to a list of pattern matching cases. Patterns are evaluated on a message, starting from the first pattern and moving down in the list of patterns. If a pattern matches, the matching message is removed from the mailbox, and subsequent patterns are not evaluated on the message. If no match is found, the message is left in the mailbox.

In this example, ChatRoom expects either a Subscribe, Unsubscribe, or UserPost message. Upon receiving any such message, ChatRoom evaluates the expression on the right side of the pattern's rocket symbol (=>).

The Scala actors library also provides a shorthand for defining and starting an actor in a single step without extending the Actor trait. Listing 4.4 shows how to rewrite the code of Listing 4.3 using the shorthand notation.

Handling subscription messages

Upon receiving a Subscribe message, a ChatRoom must add the user to its subscribers session. At first, it may seem convenient to keep chat room subscribers in a list of Users. Note, however, that subscribers must be able to receive messages from the chat room. In our current design, when a UserPost

```
val chatRoom =
  actor {
    while (true) {
      receive {
        case Subscribe(user) =>
        case Unsubscribe(user) =>
        case UserPost(user, post) =>
      }
    }
  }
```

Listing 4.4 · Creating and starting an actor with `actor`

arrives, ChatRoom iterates through its subscribers session, and sends the message's content to all subscribing users, except to the user that originally sent the message.

To enable users to accept messages from ChatRoom, you can represent each user as an actor inside the subscriber session. When ChatRoom receives a Subscribe message, it creates a new actor representing the user, and associates the user with the newly created actor. That actor, in turn, will process Post messages sent to it from the chat room; this is shown in Listing 4.5.

4.3 Sending actor messages

At this point, ChatRoom is ready to process subscription messages, so let's send some messages to it. Scala's actors library supports both asynchronous and synchronous message sending.

Asynchronous message sending

You send a message *asynchronously* to an actor with the bang (!) symbol. In using ! to denote message sending, Scala follows the tradition of Erlang:

```
val chatRoom = new ChatRoom
chatRoom ! Subscribe(User("Bob"))
```

The ! method sends a message to chatRoom and returns immediately; it doesn't wait for any confirmation or reply from the target actor. In addition

49

```scala
var session = Map.empty[User, Actor]
while (true) {
  receive {
    case Subscribe(user) =>
      val sessionUser =
        actor {
          while (true) {
            self.receive {
              case Post(msg) => // Send message to sender
            }
          }
        }
      session = session + (user -> sessionUser)

      // handle UserPost message
      // handle Unsubscribe message
  }
}
```

Listing 4.5 · Representing a user as an actor inside a session

to the message, ! also sends an implicit reference to the sender to the target actor. That reference is always available inside the target actor via the sender variable.

Listing 4.6 illustrates how the target actor uses the sender reference to process a Post message.

Note that there are *two* actors in the above example: ChatRoom and the actor representing the user inside the chat room, sessionUser. When the chat room actor receives a Subscribe message, it assigns that message's sender to the subscriber variable. The closure passed to the actor method, in turn, captures that variable and allows the subscriberActor to receive and process Post messages. Once sessionUser is initialized to the actor representing the user, it is saved away in the session map.

Synchronous messages

Scala also supports *synchronous* message sending via the !? operator:

```
var session = Map.empty[User, Actor]
while (true) {
  receive {
    case Subscribe(user) =>
      val subscriber = sender
      val sessionUser =
        actor {
          while (true) {
            self.receive {
              case Post(msg) => subscriber ! Post(msg)
            }
          }
        }
      session = session + (user -> sessionUser)
    // handle UserPost message
    // handle Unsubscribe message
  }
}
```

Listing 4.6 · Using the **sender** reference

```
val chatRoom = new ChatRoom
chatRoom !? Subscribe(User("Bob"))
```

Unlike with asynchronous message sending, !? blocks the calling thread until the message is sent and a reply received. Listing 4.7 shows how ChatRoom might return an acknowledgment when handling a subscription message with the reply method.

The client can capture and process the reply:

```
chatRoom !? Subscribe(User("Bob")) match {
  case response: String => println(response)
}
```

```scala
var session = Map.empty[User, Actor]
while (true) {
  receive {
    case Subscribe(user) =>
      val subscriber = sender
      val sessionUser =
      actor {
        while (true) {
          self.receive {
            case Post(msg) => subscriber ! Post(msg)
          }
        }
      }
      session = session + (user -> sessionUser)
      reply("Subscribed " + user)
  }
}
```

Listing 4.7 · Using the `reply` method

Futures

In some cases, you want the calling thread to return immediately after sending a message, but you may also need access to the target actor's reply at a later time. For instance, you may want to quickly return from sending a subscription message, but also record the chat room's acknowledgment message in the future.

Scala actors provide the concept of *futures* for such a scenario. Futures messages are sent with the `!!` method, which returns a `Future` without blocking the calling thread. The caller may or may not evaluate a future's value; if it does, and if the future value is not yet available, the calling thread will block:

```scala
val future = chatRoom !! Subscribe(User("Bob"))
// Do useful work
println(future()) // Wait for the future
```

Message timeouts

In the examples so far, `receive` blocks the actor's main thread until a matching message is found. In some cases, you may want to wait for suitable messages only for a certain period of time. The `receiveWithin` method allows you to specify a message timeout, and to be notified if no message was received within that time.

You can use the `receiveWithin` method to automatically unsubscribe a user if the user hasn't received a post message within a specified amount of time. In the following example, TIMEOUT will match if no Post message is received within three minutes; the user is then unsubscribed from the chat room, as Listing 4.8 shows.

```
val sessionUser = actor {
  while (true) {
    self.receiveWithin (1800 * 1000) {
      case Post(msg) => subscriber ! Post(msg)
      case TIMEOUT =>
        room ! Unsubscribe(user)
        self.exit()
    }
  }
}
```

Listing 4.8 · Using message timeouts with `receiveWithin`

Processing user posts

All that remains from our chat room to be fully functional is to implement the processing of a user's post, as shown in Listing 4.9.

```scala
var session = Map.empty[User, Actor]
def act() {
  while (true) {
    receive {
      case UserPost(user, msg) =>
        for (key <- session.keys; if key != user) {
          session(key) ! msg
        }
      // Handle Subscribe message
      // Handle Unsubscribe message
    }
  }
}
```

Listing 4.9 · Processing post messages

Chapter 5

Event-Based Programming

The constructs we introduced in Chapter 4 tie each actor to a JVM thread: each actor needs its own dedicated Java thread. The thread-per-actor approach works well if your program requires relatively few actors.

If you anticipate many actors, however, or if the number of actors in your program varies depending on input, defining one thread per actor incurs significant overhead. Not only does each JVM thread require memory for its execution stack, which is usually pre-allocated, each JVM thread may be mapped to an underlying operating system process. Depending on the platform, context-switching between those processes may involve switching between kernel and user modes, an expensive operation.

To allow many actors in a JVM, you can make your actors *event-based*. Event-based actors are implemented as event handlers instead of as threads, and are therefore more lightweight than their thread-based cousins. Since event-based actors are not tied to Java threads, event-based actors can execute on a pool of a small number of worker threads. Typically, such a pool should contain as many worker threads as there are processor cores in the system. That maximizes parallelism while keeping the overhead of pool threads—memory consumption and context-switching—to a minimum.

5.1 Events versus threads

Making an actor event-based is not entirely transparent to the programmer, because event-based programming follows a different paradigm from programming with threads. A typical actor spends some time waiting for incoming messages, and a key difference between event-based and thread-based actors can be illustrated by an actor's waiting strategy.

A thread-based actor waits by invoking `wait` on an object for which its thread holds the associated lock. That thread resumes whenever another thread invokes `notify` (or `notifyAll`) on the same object.[1] An event-based actor, by contrast, registers an event handler with the actor runtime. After that registration, the actor's computation usually finishes, and the thread initially running the computation is free to execute other tasks, or go to sleep if there is nothing else to do. Later, when an event of interest is fired—when a message of interest to the actor is received, for instance—the actor runtime schedules the actor's event handler for execution on a thread pool, and the actor's computation resumes. In that manner, event-based actors are decoupled from underlying JVM threads.

5.2 Making actors event-based: `react`

Although event-based actors differ from thread-based actors in their waiting strategies, turning a thread-based actor into an event-based one is often straightforward. The thread-based actors we have seen so far used `receive` to wait for a matching message to arrive in their mailbox. To make an actor event-based, replace all uses of `receive` by invoking the `react` method. As with `receive`, `react` expects a block of message patterns that are associated with actions to process a matching message.

Although replacing `receive` with `react` is a simple code change, there are important differences in how `receive` and `react` can be used in programs. The following examples explore these differences.

Using react to wait for messages

Listing 5.1 shows the definition of a method that recursively builds a chain of actors and returns the first actor. Each actor in the chain uses `react` to wait for a `'Die` message. When it receives such a message, the actor checks to see if it is last in the chain (in this case, `next == null`). The last actor in the chain simply responds with `'Ack` to the sender of the `'Die` message and terminates.

---

[1] In practice, waiting is slightly more complicated, because threads may be interrupted during waiting.

```
def buildChain(size: Int, next: Actor): Actor = {
  val a = actor {
    react {
      case 'Die =>
        val from = sender
        if (next != null) {
          next ! 'Die
          react {
            case 'Ack => from ! 'Ack
          }
        } else from ! 'Ack
    }
  }
  if (size > 0) buildChain(size - 1, a)
  else a
}
```

Listing 5.1 · Building a chain of event-based actors.

If the current actor is not the last in the chain, it sends a 'Die message to the next actor, and waits for an 'Ack message. When the 'Ack arrives, it notifies the original sender of the 'Die and terminates. Note that we store the sender of the original 'Die message in the local variable from, so that we can refer to this actor inside the nested react. Inside the nested react, sender refers to the next actor in the chain, whereas the current actor should send its 'Ack to the previous actor in the chain, which is stored in from.

Let's use the buildChain method by putting it into an object with the main method shown in Listing 5.2. We store the first command-line argument in the numActors variable to control the size of the actor chain. Just for fun, we take the time to see how long it takes to build and terminate a single chain of size numActors. After building the chain using buildChain, we immediately send a 'Die message to the first actor in the chain.

What happens is that each actor sends 'Die to the next actor, waiting for an 'Ack message. When the 'Ack is received, the actor propagates it to the previous actor and terminates; the first actor is the last one to receive its 'Ack. When the receive operation in the main method starts processing 'Ack, all actors in the chain have terminated.

57

```
def main(args: Array[String]) {
  val numActors = args(0).toInt
  val start = System.currentTimeMillis
  buildChain(numActors, null) ! 'Die
  receive {
    case 'Ack =>
      val end = System.currentTimeMillis
      println("Took " + (end - start) + " ms")
  }
}
```

Listing 5.2 · The main method.

Note that in the main method we cannot replace `receive` by `react`. The reason is that the main thread (the JVM thread executing the main method) should not terminate before it receives an 'Ack response. If you would use `react`, its message handler would be registered with the actor runtime, and then the main thread would terminate. When the main thread terminates, all other threads marked as daemons, including the threads of the actor runtime, are terminated, too. This means that the entire application would terminate! To avoid this problem, *use `react` only inside an actor.*

How many actors are too many?

Actors that use `react` for receiving messages are lightweight compared to normal JVM threads. Let's find out just how lightweight by creating chains of actors of ever increasing size until the JVM runs out of memory. Moreover, we can compare that chain with thread-based actors by replacing the two `react`s with `receive`s.

But first, how many event-based actors can we create? And how much time does it take to create them? On a test system, a chain of 1,000 actors is built and terminated in about 115 milliseconds, while creating and destroying a chain of 10,000 actors takes about 540 milliseconds. Building a chain with 500,000 actors takes 6,232 milliseconds, but one with 1 million actors takes a little longer: about 26 seconds without increasing the default heap size of the JVM (Java HotSpot Server VM 1.6.0).

Let's try this now with thread-based actors. Since we are going to create lots of threads, we should configure the actor runtime to avoid unreasonable overheads.

Configuring the actor runtime's thread pool

Since we intend to use lots of threads with thread-bound actors, it is more efficient to create those threads in advance. Moreover, we can adjust the size of the actor runtime's internal thread pool to optimize actor execution. Scala's actor runtime allows its thread pool to resize itself according to the number of actors blocked in `receive` (each of those actors needs its own thread), but that resizing may take a long time since the thread pool is not optimized to handle massive resizing efficiently.

We can configure the internal thread pool using two JVM properties, `actors.corePoolSize` and `actors.maxPoolSize`. The first property sets the number of pool threads that are started when the thread pool is initialized. The latter property specifies an upper bound on the total number of threads the thread pool will ever use. (The default is 256.)

To minimize the time it takes to resize the thread pool, we set both properties close to the actual number of threads that our application needs. For example, when running our chain example with 1,000 thread-based actors, setting `actors.corePoolSize` to 1,000 and `actors.maxPoolSize` to, say, 1,010 keeps the pool resizing overhead low.

With these settings in place, it takes about 12 seconds to create and destroy a chain of 1,000 thread-based actors. A chain of 2,000 threaded actors takes already more than 97 seconds. With a chain of 3,000 actors, the test JVM crashes with an `java.lang.OutOfMemoryError`.

As this simple performance test demonstrates, event-based actors are much more lightweight than thread-based actors. By running a large number of event-based actors on a small number of threads, the context-switching overhead and the resource consumption of thread-bound actors is reduced dramatically. The following sections explore how to program with event-based actors effectively.

Using react effectively

As we mentioned previously, with `react` an actor waits for a message in an event-based manner. Under the hood, instead of blocking the underlying worker thread, `react`'s block of pattern-action pairs is registered as an event handler. The actor runtime then invokes that event handler when a matching message arrives.

The event handler is all that is retained before the actor goes to sleep. In particular, the call stack, as the current thread maintains it, is discarded when the actor suspends. This enables the runtime system to release the underlying worker thread, so that it can be reused to execute other actors.

Exceptions and react

Code surrounding an invocation of react should never catch instances of java.lang.Throwable. Doing so would interfere with internal exceptions used for flow control. By contrast, catching instances of (subtypes of) java.lang.Exception is always safe.

The fact that the current thread's call stack is discarded when an event-based actor suspends bears an important consequence on the event-based actor programming model: a call to react never returns normally. Instead, react always throws an internal control exception, which the actor runtime handles. Like any Scala or Java method, react could return normally only if its full call stack was available when it executed. Since that isn't the case with event-based actors, a call to react never returns.

The fact that react never returns means that no code can follow a react method invocation: Since react doesn't return, code following react would never execute. Thus, invoking react must always be the last thing an event-based actor does before it terminates. For example, in Listing 5.3 the actor won't print "finished" since it follows the call to react. This problem is corrected by moving the expression that prints "finished" into the body of the react call, as shown in Listing 5.4.

Since an actor's main job is to handle interesting messages, and since react defines an event-based message-handling mechanism for actors, you might think that react will always be the last, and even only, thing an actor needs to do. However, it is sometimes convenient to perform several react invocations in succession. In those situations, you could nest react invocations in sequence, as we saw in Listing 5.1.

Alternatively, you could define a recursive method that calls react several times in sequence. For instance, we can extend our simple chain example so that an actor waits for a specified number of 'Die messages before it

```
actor {
  react {
    case "hello" =>
      println("hi")
  }
  println("finished")
}
```

Listing 5.3 · Incorrect use of react.

```
actor {
  react {
    case "hello" =>
      println("hi")
      println("finished")
  }
}
```

Listing 5.4 · Correct use of react.

terminates. Listing 5.5 shows how to do this by replacing the body of the chain actors with a call to the waitFor method. The waitFor method tests up front whether the current actor should terminate (if n == 0) or continue waiting for messages. The protocol logic is the same as before. The only difference is that after each message sends to from, we added a recursive call to waitFor.

Composing react-based code with combinators

Sometimes it is difficult or impossible to use recursive methods for sequencing multiple reacts, which is the case when reusing classes and methods that use react. By their nature, reusable components cannot be changed after they have been built. In particular, we cannot simply perform invasive changes, such as when we added iteration through a recursive method in the example in Listing 5.5. This section illustrates several ways in which we can reuse react-based code.

For example, suppose our project contains the sleep method shown in Listing 5.6. It registers the current actor, self, with a timer service (not

```
def waitFor(n: Int): Unit = if (n > 0) {
  react {
    case 'Die =>
      val from = sender
      if (next != null) {
        next ! 'Die
        react {
          case 'Ack => from ! 'Ack; waitFor(n - 1)
        }
      } else { from ! 'Ack; waitFor(n - 1) }
  }
}
```

Listing 5.5 · Sequencing `react` calls using a recursive method.

Recursive methods and `react`

You might be concerned that calling a recursive method as Listing 5.5 does could quickly lead to a stack overflow. The good news, however, is that `react` plays extremely well with recursive methods: whenever an invocation of `react` resumes due to a matching message in the actor's mailbox, a task item is created and submitted to the actor runtime's internal thread pool for execution. The thread that executes that task item doesn't have much else on its call stack, apart from the basic logic of being a pool worker thread. As a result, every invocation of `react` executes on a call stack that is as good as empty. The call stack of a recursive method like `waitFor` in Listing 5.5, therefore, doesn't grow at all thanks to the `react` invocations.

---

shown) to wake it up after the specified `delay`, which is provided as a parameter. The `timer` notifies the registered actor using an `'Awake` message. For efficiency, `sleep` uses `react` to wait for the `'Awake` so that the sleeping actor does not require the resources of a JVM thread while it is sleeping.

Using the `sleep` method shown in Listing 5.6 invariably requires executing something after its `react` invocation. However, since we want to reuse the method as is, we cannot simply insert something in the body of its `react`. Instead, we need a way to combine the `sleep` method with the

```
def sleep(delay: Long) {
  register(timer, delay, self)
  react { case 'Awake => /* OK, continue */ }
}
```

Listing 5.6 · A sleep method that uses react.

code that should run after the 'Awake message has been received *without changing the implementation of sleep.*

That is where the Actor object's control-flow combinators come into play. These combinators let you express common communication patterns in a relatively simple and concise way. The most basic combinator is andThen. The andThen combinator combines two code blocks to run after each other even if the first one invokes react.

Listing 5.7 shows how you can use andThen to execute code that runs after invoking the sleep method. You use andThen as an operator that is written infix between two blocks of code. The first block of code invokes sleep as its last action, which, in turn, invokes react.

```
actor {
  val period = 1000
  {
    // code before going to sleep
    sleep(period)
  } andThen {
    // code after waking up
  }
}
```

Listing 5.7 · Using andThen to continue after react.

Note that the period parameter of sleep is declared outside the code block on which andThen operates. This is possible because the two code blocks are actually *closures* that may capture variables in their environment. The second block of code is run when the react of the first code block (the one inside sleep) is finished. However, note that the second code block is really the last thing the actor executes. Using andThen does not change the fact that react invocations do not return. andThen merely allows you to

63

combine two pieces of code in sequence.

Another useful combinator is loopWhile. As its name suggests, it loops running a provided closure while some condition holds. Thanks to Scala's flexible syntax, loopWhile feels almost like a native language primitive. Listing 5.8 shows a variation of our actor chain example that uses loopWhile to wait for multiple 'Die messages. Again, we make use of the fact that the two code block parameters of loopWhile, the condition (n > 0) and the body, are closures, since both code blocks access the local variable n. (Each actor instance will wait for lives 'Die events before actually giving up the ghost.) Note that the top-level react in the body of loopWhile is unchanged from the first example that did not support iteration. You might as well extract the body to a method—loopWhile works in either case.

```scala
def buildChain(size: Int, next: Actor, lives: Int): Actor = {
  val a = actor {
    var n = lives
    loopWhile (n > 0) {
      n -= 1
      react {
        case 'Die =>
          val from = sender
          if (next != null) {
            next ! 'Die
            react { case 'Ack => from ! 'Ack }
          } else from ! 'Ack
      }
    }
  }
  if (size > 0) buildChain(size - 1, a, lives)
  else a
}
```

Listing 5.8 · Using loopWhile for iterations with react.

5.3 Event-based futures

In Chapter 4, we illustrated how to use futures for result-bearing messages. Some of the methods used to wait for the result of a future rely on the thread-based `receive` under the hood. While waiting for the result, those methods monopolize the underlying worker thread. We can also wait for a future in an event-based way with `react`.

For example, suppose we want to render a summary of all images linked from a web page at a given URL. We can render each image individually once the image has finished downloading. To increase the application's throughput, each image is downloaded by its own actor. Since each downloading actor performs a result-bearing task, it is convenient to use futures to keep track of the expected results. Listing 5.9 shows the code for rendering images in this way.

```
def renderImages(url: String) {
  val imageInfos = scanForImageInfo(url)
  val dataFutures = for (info <- imageInfos) yield {
    val loader = actor {
      react { case Download(info) =>
        reply(info.downloadImage())
      }
    }
    loader !! Download(info)
  }
  for (i <- 0 until imageInfos.size) {
    dataFutures(i)() match {
      case data @ ImageData(_) =>
        renderImage(data)
    }
  }
  println("OK, all images rendered.")
}
```

Listing 5.9 · Image renderer using futures.

First, the `renderImages` method scans the URL, provided as a parameter, for image information. For each image, we start a new actor that

65

downloads the image and replies with image data. We obtain a future using the !! message send variant. Once all the futures have been collected in dataFutures, the current actor waits for each future by invoking the future's apply method.[2]

Example: image renderer with react and futures

In the implementation we just described, the underlying thread blocks while waiting for a future. However, we can also wait for a future in a non-blocking, event-based way using react. The key for this to work is the InputChannel associated with each Future instance. We use this channel to transmit the result of the future to the actor that created the future. Invoking a future's apply method waits to receive the result on that channel, using the thread-based receive. However, we can also wait for the results in an event-based way using react on the future's InputChannel.

Listing 5.10 shows an implementation that does just that. Since we need to invoke react several times in sequence, you have to use one of the control-flow combinators of Section 5.2. In this example, we use loopWhile to emulate the indexing scheme of the previous version in Listing 5.9. The main difference is that in this implementation the index variable i is declared and incremented explicitly, and the generator in the for-expresssion has been replaced with a termination condition.

You can also build custom control-flow combinators that allow you to use react inside for-expresssions. In the following section, we explain how you can do this.

Building custom control-flow operators

Sometimes the existing control-flow combinators that the Actor object provides are not well-suited for the task at hand. In such cases, building custom control-flow operators can help. In this section, you will learn how you can use the control-flow combinators that the Actor object provides to build custom operators that let you use react (and methods using react) inside for expressions.

---

[2]Scala provides a shorthand syntax for invoking apply methods. To invoke an apply method, it suffices to add the parameter list directly after the receiver. For example, fut() is equivalent to fut.apply().

```
def renderImages(url: String) {
  val imageInfos = scanForImageInfo(url)
  val dataFutures = for (info <- imageInfos) yield {
    val loader = actor {
      react { case Download(info) =>
        reply(info.downloadImage())
      }
    }
    loader !! Download(info)
  }
  var i = 0
  loopWhile (i < imageInfos.size) {
    i += 1
    dataFutures(i-1).inputChannel.react {
      case data @ ImageData(_) => renderImage(data)
    }
  } andThen { println("OK, all images rendered.") }
}
```

Listing 5.10 · Using react to wait for futures.

Listing 5.11 illustrates how to use a custom ForEach operator that allows you to iterate over a list while invoking react for each element in the list. In this case, we want to iterate over the futures in dataFutures. We use ForEach to convert the plain dataFutures list into an object that acts as a generator in for expressions. It generates the same values as the dataFutures list, namely all of the list's elements. However, it does so in a way that allows continuing the iteration even after react is invoked inside the body of the for expressions.

Listing 5.12 shows the implementation of ForEach. Making ForEach a case class allows you to omit new when creating new instances. The constructor takes a parameter of type Iterable[T]—the collection that generates the elements for our iteration.

The ForEach class has a single method foreach that takes a parameter of function type T => Unit. Implementing the foreach method enables instances of the ForEach class to be used as generators in simple for expressions, like the one in Listing 5.11. The variable that is bound to the generated

```
def renderImages(url: String) {
  val imageInfos = scanForImageInfo(url)
  val dataFutures = for (info <- imageInfos) yield {
    val loader = actor {
      react { case Download(info) =>
        reply(info.downloadImage())
      }
    }
    loader !! Download(info)
  }
  {
    for (ft <- ForEach(dataFutures)) {
      ft.inputChannel.react {
        case data @ ImageData(_) => renderImage(data)
      }
    }
  } andThen {
    println("OK, all images rendered.")
  }
}
```

Listing 5.11 · Enabling react in for expressions.

```
case class ForEach[T](iter: Iterable[T]) {
  def foreach(fun: T => Unit): Unit = {
    val it = iter.elements
    loopWhile (it.hasNext) {
      fun(it.next)
    }
  }
}
```

Listing 5.12 · Implementing the custom ForEach operator.

elements in the `for` expression corresponds to the parameter of the function `fun`. The body of the `for` expression corresponds to the body of `fun`.

Inside `foreach`, we first obtain an iterator, `it`, from the `Iterable`. Then, we iterate over the collection using `it` and the `loopWhile` combinator introduced in Section 5.2. In each iteration, we apply the parameter function `fun` to the current element of the collection. Since we are using `loopWhile`, it is safe to invoke `react` inside `fun`.

Chapter 6

Exceptions, Actor Termination, and Shutdown

In this chapter, we will look at how to handle errors in concurrent, actor-based programs. Actors provide several additional ways to handle exceptions compared to sequential Scala code. In particular, we will show how an actor can handle exceptions that are thrown but not handled by other actors. More generally, we will look at ways in which an actor can monitor other actors to detect whether they terminated normally or abnormally (for instance, through an unhandled exception). Finally, we introduce several concepts and techniques that can simplify termination management of actor-based programs.

6.1   Simple exception handling

An actor terminates automatically when an exception that is not handled inside the actor's body is thrown. One possible symptom of such a situation is that other actors wait indefinitely for messages from the dead actor. Since, by default, terminating actors do not generate any feedback, it can be quite time-consuming to find out what happened and why.

The way to guard against actors that silently terminate because of unhandled exceptions is to invoke a global exception handler whenever an exception propagates out of the actor's body. You can do this by subclassing `Actor` (or its super-trait `Reactor`, which will be described in Chapter 11) and overriding its `exceptionHandler` member. It is defined as follows (omitting the method's modifiers):

71

```
def exceptionHandler: PartialFunction[Exception, Unit]
```

As you can see, a parameterless method returns a partial function that you can apply to instances of java.lang.Exception. Whenever an exception that would normally cause the actor to terminate is thrown inside an actor's body, the runtime system checks whether the actor's exceptionHandler matches the given exception. If so, the exceptionHandler partial function is applied to the exception. After that, the actor terminates normally.

```
object A extends Actor {
  def act() {
    react {
      case 'hello =>
        throw new Exception("Error!")
    }
  }
  override def exceptionHandler = {
    case e: Exception =>
      println(e.getMessage())
  }
}
```

Listing 6.1 · Defining an actor-global exception handler.

Listing 6.1 shows how to override the exceptionHandler method so that it returns a custom partial function. The actor itself handles a single message consisting of the Symbol 'hello.[1] Let's interact with the A actor using Scala's interpreter shell:

```
scala> A.start()
res0: scala.actors.Actor = A$@1ea414e

scala> A ! 'hello
Error!
```

As expected, A's overridden exceptionHandler method runs, printing the message string attached to the thrown exception, which is just "Error!".

---

[1] In Scala, Symbols are similar to strings, except that they are always interned, which makes equality checks fast. Also, the syntax for creating Symbols is slightly more lightweight compared to strings.

This form of exception handling using `exceptionHandler` works well together with control-flow combinators, such as `loop`. You can use the combinators to resume the normal execution of an actor after handling an exception. For example, let's modify the A actor's `act` method in Listing 6.1 as follows:

```scala
def act() {
  var lastMsg: Option[Symbol] = None
  loopWhile (lastMsg.isEmpty || lastMsg.get != 'stop) {
    react {
      case 'hello =>
        throw new Exception("Error!")
      case any: Symbol =>
        println("your message: " + any)
        lastMsg = Some(any)
    }
  }
}
```

The invocation of `react` is now wrapped inside a `loopWhile` that tests whether the last received message is equal to `'stop`, in which case the actor terminates. Now, if the actor receives a `'hello` message, it throws the exception, which is handled as before. However, instead of terminating, the actor simply resumes its execution by continuing with the next loop iteration. This means that the actor is ready to receive more messages after the exception has been handled.

Let's try this out in the interpreter:

```scala
scala> A.start()
res0: scala.actors.Actor = A$@1cb048e

scala> A ! 'hello
Error!

scala> A.getState
res2: scala.actors.Actor.State.Value = Suspended

scala> A ! 'hi
your message: 'hi

scala> A ! 'stop
your message: 'stop
```

73

```
scala> A.getState
res5: scala.actors.Actor.State.Value = Terminated
```

Note that after sending 'hello the actor eventually suspends waiting for the next message. You can use the getState method to query an actor's execution state. It returns values of the Actor.State enumeration, which is defined in the Actor object. The Suspended state indicates that the actor has invoked react and is now waiting for a matching message. Therefore, we can continue to interact with the actor by sending it a 'hi message. After the actor receives a 'stop message, its loopWhile loop finishes and the actor terminates normally. The final state value is Terminated.

6.2   Monitoring actors

There are several scenarios in which you need to monitor the life cycle of a group of actors. In particular, you can significantly simplify error handling and fault tolerance in a concurrent system through monitoring. Here are some examples:

Scenario A. We want to be notified when an actor terminates normally or abnormally. For instance, we might want to replace an actor that terminated because of an unhandled exception. Or we might want to rethrow the exception in a different actor that can handle it.

Scenario B. We want to express that an actor *depends* on some other actor in the sense that the former cannot function without the latter. For instance, in a typical master-slave architecture the work that a slave does is useless if the master has crashed. In this case, it would be desirable if all slaves would terminate automatically whenever the master crashes to avoid needless consumption of resources, such as memory.

Both of the above scenarios require us to monitor an actor's life cycle. In particular, they require us to be notified when an actor terminates, normally or abnormally. The actors package provides special support for managing such notifications. However, before diving into those monitoring constructs it is helpful to look at the ways in which actors can terminate.

Actor termination

There are three reasons why an actor terminates:

1. The actor finishes executing the body of its `act` method.

2. The actor invokes `exit`.

3. An exception propagates out of the actor's body.

The first reason is a special case of the second one: After executing an actor's body, the runtime system invokes `exit` implicitly on the terminating actor. The `exit` method can be invoked with or without passing an argument.

The `Actor` trait contains the following two method definitions (omitting the modifiers):

```
def exit(): Nothing
def exit(reason: AnyRef): Nothing
```

Both methods have result type `Nothing`, which means that invocations do not return normally because an exception is thrown in all cases. In this case, the particular instance of `Throwable` should never be caught inside the actor, since it is used for internal life-cycle control. Invoking `exit` (with or without argument) terminates the current actor's execution. The `reason` parameter is supposed to indicate the reason for terminating the actor. Invoking `exit` without an argument is equivalent to passing the `Symbol 'normal` to `exit`; it indicates that the actor terminated normally. Examples for arguments that indicate abnormal termination are:

- Exceptions that the actor cannot handle

- Message objects that the actor cannot process

- Invalid user input

Exceptions that propagate out of an actor's body lead to that actor's abnormal termination. In the following section, you will learn how actors can react to the termination of other actors. We will show the difference between normal and abnormal termination as seen from an outside actor. More importantly, we will see how to obtain the exit reason of another actor that terminated abnormally.

Linking actors

An actor that wants to receive notifications when another actor terminates must *link* itself to the other actor. Actors that are linked together implicitly monitor each other.

For example, Listing 6.2 shows a slave actor, which is supposed to do work on behalf of a master actor. The work that the slave does is useless without the master, since the master manages all results produced by the slave—the slave *depends* on its master. This means that whenever the master crashes, its dependent slave should terminate, since otherwise it would only needlessly consume resources. This is where *links* come into play. Using the link method, the slave actor links itself to the master actor to express the fact that it depends on it. As a result, the slave is notified whenever its master terminates.

```scala
object Master extends Actor {
  def act() {
    Slave ! 'doWork
    react {
      case 'done =>
        throw new Exception("Master crashed")
    }
  }
}
object Slave extends Actor {
  def act() {
    link(Master)
    loop {
      react {
        case 'doWork =>
          println("Done")
          reply('done)
      }
    }
  }
}
```

Listing 6.2 · Linking dependent actors.

By default, termination notifications are not delivered as messages to the mailbox of the notified actor. Instead, they have the following effect:

- If the terminating actor's exit reason is 'normal, no action is taken.

- If the terminating actor's exit reason is different from 'normal, the notified actor automatically terminates with the same exit reason.

In our master-slave example, this means that the master actor's termination, which the unhandled exception causes, results in the slave actor's termination; the exit reason of the slave actor is the same as for the master actor, namely an instance of UncaughtException. The purpose of class UncaughtException is to provide information about the context in which the exception was thrown, such as the actor, the last message that actor processed, and the sender of that message. The next section shows how to use that information effectively.

Let's use the interpreter shell to interact with the two actors:

```
scala> Slave.start()
res0: scala.actors.Actor = Slave$@190c99

scala> Slave.getState
res1: scala.actors.Actor.State.Value = Suspended

scala> Master.start()
Done
res2: scala.actors.Actor = Master$@395aaf

scala> Master.getState
res3: scala.actors.Actor.State.Value = Terminated

scala> Slave.getState
res4: scala.actors.Actor.State.Value = Terminated
```

Right after starting the Slave, its state is Suspended. When the Master starts, it sends a 'doWork request to its Slave, which prints Done to the console and replies to the Master with 'done. Once the Master receives 'done, it throws an unhandled exception causing it to terminate abnormally. Because of the link between Slave and Master, this causes the Slave to terminate automatically. Therefore, both actors are in state Terminated at the end.

Trapping termination notifications. In some cases, it is useful to receive termination notifications as messages in a monitoring actor's mailbox. For example, a monitoring actor may want to rethrow an exception that isn't handled by some linked actor. Or, it may want to react to normal termination, which is not possible by default.

You can configure actors to receive all termination notifications as normal messages in their mailbox using the Boolean `trapExit` flag. In the following example, actor b links itself to actor a:

```
val a = actor { ... }
val b = actor {
  self.trapExit = true
  link(a)
  ...
}
```

Note that before actor b invokes `link` it sets its `trapExit` member to `true`; this means that whenever a linked actor terminates (normally or abnormally) it receives a message of type `Exit` (see below). Therefore, actor b is going to be notified whenever actor a terminates (assuming that actor a did not terminate before b's invocation of `link`).

Listing 6.3 makes this more concrete by having actor a throw an exception. The exception causes a to terminate, resulting in an `Exit` message to actor b. Running it produces the following output:

```
Actor 'a' terminated because of UncaughtException(...)
```

`Exit` is a case class with the following parameters:

```
case class Exit(from: AbstractActor, reason: AnyRef)
```

The first parameter tells us which actor has terminated. In Listing 6.3, actor b uses a guard in the message pattern to only react to `Exit` messages indicating that actor a has terminated. The second parameter of the `Exit` case class indicates the reason why actor `from` has terminated.

The termination of a linked actor that some unhandled exception caused results in an `Exit` message in which `reason` is equal to an instance of `UncaughtException`; it is a case class with the following fields:

• `actor: Actor`: the actor that threw the uncaught exception

```
val a = actor {
  react {
    case 'start =>
      val somethingBadHappened = true
      if (somethingBadHappened)
        throw new Exception("Error!")
      println("Nothing bad happened")
  }
}
val b = actor {
  self.trapExit = true
  link(a)
  a ! 'start
  react {
    case Exit(from, reason) if from == a =>
      println("Actor 'a' terminated because of " + reason)
  }
}
```

Listing 6.3 · Receiving a notification because of an unhandled exception.

- message: Option[Any]: the (optional) message the actor was processing; None if the actor did not receive a message

- sender: Option[OutputChannel[Any]]: the (optional) sender of
  the most recently processed message

- cause: Throwable: the exception that caused the actor to terminate

Since UncaughtException is a case class, it can be matched against
when receiving an Exit message. For instance, in Listing 6.3 we can extract the exception that caused actor a to terminate directly from the Exit
message:

```
react {
  case Exit(from, UncaughtException(_, _, _, _, cause))
       if from == a =>
    println("Actor 'a' terminated because of " + cause)
}
```

79

Running Listing 6.3 with the above change results in the following output:

```
Actor 'a' terminated because of java.lang.Exception: Error!
```

When an actor's `trapExit` member is `true`, the actor is also notified when a linked actor terminates normally; for instance, when it finishes the execution of its body. In this case, the `Exit` message's `reason` field is the `Symbol 'normal`. You can try this yourself by changing the local variable `somethingBadHappened` to `false`. The output of running the code should then look like this:

```
Nothing bad happened
Actor 'a' terminated because of 'normal
```

Restarting crashed actors

In some cases, it is useful to restart an actor that has terminated because of an unhandled exception. By resetting a crashed actor's state, or at least parts of it, chances are that the actor can successfully process outstanding messages in its mailbox. Alternatively, upon restart the outstanding messages could be retrieved from the crashed actor's mailbox and forwarded to a healthy actor.

Listing 6.4 shows how to create a keep-alive actor that monitors another actor, restarting it whenever it crashes. The idea is that the keep-alive actor first links itself to the monitored actor (the `patient`), and then invokes `keepAlive`. The `keepAlive` method works as follows: When receiving an `Exit` message indicating the abnormal termination of `patient` (in this case, `reason != 'normal`), we re-link `self` to `patient` and restart it. Finally, `keepAlive` invokes itself recursively to continue monitoring the `patient`.

You may wonder why we link `self` to the `patient` actor before restarting it. After all, `keepAlive` assumes that this link already exists. The reason is that `self` automatically unlinks itself when receiving an `Exit` message from `patient`. We do this to avoid leaking memory through links that are never removed. Since in most cases terminated actors are not restarted, this behavior is a good default.

Listing 6.5 shows how to use our `keepAlive` method to automatically restart an actor whenever it crashes. Actor `crasher` is the actor that we want to monitor and restart. It maintains a counter such that whenever the counter is even, handling a `'request` message results in an exception being thrown. Since the exception is not handled, it causes the actor to crash. We can also

```
// assumes 'self' linked to 'patient' and 'self.trapExit == true'
def keepAlive(patient: Actor): Nothing = {
  react {
    case Exit(from, reason) if from == patient =>
      if (reason != 'normal) {
        link(patient)
        patient.restart()
        keepAlive(patient)
      }
  }
}
```

Listing 6.4 · Monitoring and restarting an actor using link and restart.

tell the crasher to stop, thereby terminating it normally. The client actor waits for a 'start message, and then sends several requests to crasher, some of which cause crashes.

The last actor, the keep-alive actor, links itself to the crasher with trapExit set to true. It is important that the keep-alive actor links itself to the crasher before the client starts. Otherwise, the client could cause the crasher to terminate without sending an Exit message to the keep-alive actor; since the Exit message would never be received, the crasher actor would not be restarted. Running the code in Listing 6.5 produces the following output:

```
I'm (re-)born
I try to service a request
I try to service a request
sometimes I crash...
I'm (re-)born
I try to service a request
I try to service a request
sometimes I crash...
I'm (re-)born
I try to service a request
I try to service a request
sometimes I crash...
I'm (re-)born
```

81

```scala
val crasher = actor {
  println("I'm (re-)born")
  var cnt = 0
  loop {
    cnt += 1
    react {
      case 'request =>
        println("I try to service a request")
        if (cnt % 2 == 0) {
          println("sometimes I crash...")
          throw new Exception
        }
      case 'stop =>
        exit()
    }
  }
}
val client = actor {
  react {
    case 'start =>
      for (_ <- 1 to 6) { crasher ! 'request }
      crasher ! 'stop
  }
}
actor {
  self.trapExit = true
  link(crasher)
  client ! 'start
  keepAlive(crasher)
}
```

Listing 6.5 · Using keepAlive to automatically restart a crashed actor.

```
def renderImages(url: String) {
  val imageInfos = scanForImageInfo(url)
  self.trapExit = true
  val dataFutures = for (info <- imageInfos) yield {
    val loader = link {
      react { case Download(info) =>
        throw new Exception("no connection")
        reply(info.downloadImage())
      }: Unit
    }
    loader !! Download(info)
  }
  var i = 0
  loopWhile (i < imageInfos.size) {
    i += 1
    val Input = dataFutures(i-1).inputChannel
    react {
      case Input ! (data @ ImageData(_)) =>
        renderImage(data)
      case Exit(from, UncaughtException(_, Some(Download(info)),
                                    _, _, cause)) =>
        println("Couldn't download image "+info+
               " because of "+cause)
    }
  }
}
```

Listing 6.6 · Reacting to Exit messages for exception handling.

As you can see, the `crasher` actor processes six `'request` messages. Every second message results in a crash, causing the keep-alive actor to restart it. Restarting the `crasher` re-runs its body, producing a rebirth message.

Exception handling using futures

One advantage of futures over simple asynchronous messages is that they make it easy to identify to which request they correspond. Basically, each future represents the asynchronous request that created the future. We can leverage this property of futures for exception handling. Let's revisit the image downloader example of Chapter 5. In the following section, we will show how you can extend Listing 5.10 to handle exceptions that may be thrown during image retrieval (for instance, `IOExceptions`).

Listing 6.6 shows the `renderImages` method extended with code to handle uncaught exceptions in the downloader actors. The idea is as follows: First, the actor that renders the images sets its `trapExit` member to `true`, which enables it to receive termination notifications from linked actors. Second, the renderer actor links itself to each downloader actor. For this, we use one of the `link` methods defined in the `Actor` object. The variant we use takes a code block (more precisely, a by-name parameter of type => Unit) as an argument, creates a new actor to execute that block, and links the caller to the newly created actor. More importantly, you link and start the new actor in a single, atomic operation to avoid a subtle race condition. Between starting the new actor and linking to it, the newly created actor could die, which would result in a lost `Exit` message. This is the main reason the `Actor` object provides a `link` method that takes a code block as an argument.

Note that you have to add an explicit type annotation to the `react` expression. The reason is that the return type of `react` is `Nothing`, which is compatible with both `link` methods since `Nothing` is a subtype of every other type. By adding the : `Unit` *type ascription*, we force the compiler to select the `link` method that takes a code block.

After the renderer actor has sent out all download requests, it loops trying to receive `ImageData` objects from each future's input channel. To handle uncaught exceptions in the downloader actors, the renderer also reacts to `Exit` messages. Whenever an `Exit` message with an `UncaughtException` as its reason is received, we use a nested pattern to extract the message the terminated actor was processing. This enables us to easily access the corresponding `ImageInfo`, since it was passed as part of the `Download` message.

Chapter 7

Customizing Actor Execution

Actors are executed using a runtime system that is backed by an efficient task execution framework. You have seen that such a runtime system enables concurrent programs to scale to a large number of fairly lightweight actors. In this chapter, you will learn how to customize the runtime system, improve the integration with threads and thread-local data, simplify testing, and more.

In Chapter 5, you saw that event-based actors require only a few worker threads to execute. However, when actors use blocking operations, the number of worker threads must often be increased to avoid locking up the thread pool. *Managed blocking* provides a way to automatically adjust the thread pool size depending on the blocking behavior of operations. In this chapter, you will learn how to use managed blocking to enable safe use of existing blocking concurrency classes.

7.1   Pluggable schedulers

In some cases, you must customize the way in which actors are executed, including when:

- Maintaining thread-bound properties such as `ThreadLocals`

- Interfacing with existing event dispatch threads

- Using daemon-style actors

- Testing with deterministic execution of message sends/receives for reproducible testing

- Maintaining fine-grained control over resources consumed by the underlying thread pool

The part of the runtime system that executes an actor's behavior is called a *scheduler*. Each actor is associated with a scheduler object that executes the actor's actions; that is, its body as well as its reactions to received messages. By default, a global scheduler executes all actors on a single thread pool. However, in principle each actor may be executed by its own scheduler.

To customize an actor's scheduler, you override the `scheduler` method inherited from the `Reactor` trait. The method returns an instance of trait `IScheduler`, which is used to execute the actor's actions. By returning a custom `IScheduler` instance, the default execution mechanism can be overridden. In the following sections, we will show you how to do this for each case listed above.

Maintaining thread-bound properties

When an application is run on the JVM, certain properties are maintained on a by-thread basis. Examples for such properties include the context class loader, the access control context, and programmer-defined `ThreadLocals`. In applications that use actors instead of threads, these properties are still useful or maybe even necessary to interoperate with JVM-based libraries and frameworks.

Using `ThreadLocals` or other thread-bound properties is done the same way as threads when using thread-based actors. For event-based actors, the situation is slightly more complicated since the underlying thread that is executing a single event-based actor may change over time. Remember that each time an actor suspends in a `react`, the underlying thread is released. When this actor resumes, it may be executed by a different thread. Thus, without some additional logic, `ThreadLocals` could change unexpectedly during an event-based actor's execution, which would be confusing. In the next section, we show you how to correctly maintain thread-bound properties, such as `ThreadLocals`, over the event-based actor's lifetime.

Example: thread-local variables

Listing 7.1 shows an attempt to use a `ThreadLocal` to track a name associated with the current actor. The name is stored in a `ThreadLocal[String]` called `tname`. In Java, `ThreadLocals` are typically declared as static class members, since they hold data that is not specific to a class instance but to an entire thread. In Scala, there are no static class members. Instead, data that is not specific to a class instance is held in singleton objects. Object members are translated to static class members in the JVM bytecode. Therefore, we declare the thread-local tname as a member of the application's object, as opposed to a member of a class or trait. We override the initialValue method to provide the initial value "john". The joeActor responds to the first 'YourName request by first setting its name to "joe jr.", and then sending it back in a reply to the sender. Upon the second 'YourName request, the thread-local name is sent back unchanged as a reply. The other actor simply sends two requests and prints their responses. We expect the program to produce the following output:

```
your name: joe jr.
your name: joe jr.
```

However, surprisingly, some executions produce the following output:

```
your name: joe jr.
your name: john
```

Apparently, in this execution the second 'YourName request returns the initial value of the ThreadLocal, even though it has been set previously by the actor to a different value. As already mentioned, the underlying problem is that parts of an event-based actor are not always executed by the same underlying thread. After resuming the second react, the actor can be executed by a thread that is different from the thread that executed the reaction to the first request. In that case, the ThreadLocal containing the initial value has not been updated yet.

We can avoid the above problem as follows: First, we create a subclass of the Actor trait that stores a copy of the thread-local variable. The idea is to restore the actual ThreadLocal using this copy whenever the actor resumes. Conversely, we save the current value of the ThreadLocal to the actor's copy whenever the actor suspends. This way, we make sure that the ThreadLocal holds the correct value while the actor executes, namely the value associated with the current actor.

The solution that we just outlined requires us to run custom code upon an actor's suspension and resumption. We can achieve this by overriding the scheduler that is used to execute the actor. However, we only want to override

87

```
object ActorWithThreadLocalWrong extends Application {
  val tname = new ThreadLocal[String] {
    override protected def initialValue() = "john"
  }
  val joeActor = actor {
    react { case 'YourName =>
      tname set "joe jr."
      sender ! tname.get
      react { case 'YourName =>
        sender ! tname.get
      }
    }
  }
  actor {
    println("your name: " + (joeActor !? 'YourName))
    println("your name: " + (joeActor !? 'YourName))
  }
}
```

Listing 7.1 · Incorrect use of ThreadLocal.

```
abstract class ActorWithThreadLocal(private var name: String)
  extends Actor {
  override val scheduler = new SchedulerAdapter {
    def execute(codeBlock: => Unit): Unit =
      ActorWithThreadLocal.super.scheduler execute {
        tname set name
        codeBlock
        name = tname.get
      }
  }
}
```

Listing 7.2 · Saving and restoring a ThreadLocal.

88

a specific method of the scheduler, namely the method that receives the code to be executed after an actor resumes and before it suspends. Since this is the most common use case when overriding an actor's scheduler, the helper trait SchedulerAdapter, allows us to override only this required method.

This implementation using SchedulerAdapter is shown in Listing 7.2. The abstract ActorWithThreadLocal class overrides the scheduler member with a new instance of a SchedulerAdapter subclass. This subclass implements the execute method that receives the code block, which is executed after this actor resumes and before it suspends. To insert the required code, we invoke the execute method of the inherited scheduler, passing a closure that surrounds the evaluation of the by-name codeBlock argument with additional code. Before the actor resumes, we restore the thread-local tname with the value of the actor's copy in its private name member. Normally, after running the code block, the actor would suspend. In our extended closure, we additionally save the current value of tname in the actor's name member before we suspend. By making joeActor in Listing 7.1 an instance of ActorWithThreadLocal, its thread-local state is managed correctly.

Interfacing with event dispatch threads

Some frameworks restrict certain actions to special threads that the framework manages. For example, a special event dispatch thread manages the event queue of Java's Swing class library. For thread safety, Swing UI components may only be accessed inside event handlers that this dispatch thread executes. Therefore, an actor that wants to interact with Swing components must run on the event dispatch thread. This is just one example where you need to "bind" actors to specific threads that are provided by some framework. Another example is a library that interacts with native code through JNI, where all accesses must be performed by a single JVM thread.

By overriding an actor's scheduler, we can ensure that its actions are executed on a specific thread, instead of an arbitrary worker thread of the actor runtime system. For this, we can again use the SchedulerAdapter trait, which we showed in the previous section. Listing 7.3 shows the implementation of an Actor subclass that executes its instances only on the Swing event dispatch thread. For this, we override the scheduler member with a new instance of a SchedulerAdapter that executes the actor's actions by submitting Runnables to the Swing event dispatch thread. We do this using the invokeLater method of java.awt.EventQueue.

```
abstract class SwingActor extends Actor {
  override val scheduler = new SchedulerAdapter {
    def execute(codeBlock: => Unit): Unit =
      java.awt.EventQueue.invokeLater(
        new Runnable() {
          def run() = codeBlock
        }
      )
  }
}
```

Listing 7.3 · Executing actors on the Swing event dispatch thread.

Daemon-style actors

In many cases, we don't have to care about the termination of an actor-based program. When all actors have finished their execution, the program terminates. However, when actors are long-running or react to messages inside an infinite loop, orderly termination of actors and the underlying thread pool can become challenging.

Some applications use actors that are always ready to accept requests to process work in the background. To simplify termination in such cases, it can help to make those actors daemons: the existence of active daemon actors does not prevent the main program from terminating. This means that as soon as all non-daemon actors have terminated, the application terminates.

Listing 7.4 shows how to create actors with daemon-style semantics: simply override the scheduler method to return the DaemonScheduler object. DaemonScheduler uses the exact same configuration as the default Scheduler object, except that the actors that it manages do not prevent the application from terminating. In Listing 7.4 the d actor is again waiting for a message after the synchronous send has been served. However, since the main thread finishes, the DaemonScheduler also terminates, and with it the d actor.

Deterministic actor execution

By default, the execution of concurrent actors is not deterministic. This means that two actors that are ready to react to a received message may

```scala
import scala.actors.Actor
import scala.actors.scheduler.DaemonScheduler

object DaemonActors {

  class MyDaemon extends Actor {
    override def scheduler = DaemonScheduler
    def act() {
      loop {
        react { case num: Int => reply(num + 1) }
      }
    }
  }

  def main(args: Array[String]) {
    val d = (new MyDaemon).start()
    println(d !? 41)
  }
}
```

Listing 7.4 · Creating daemon-style actors.

be executed in any order, or, depending on the number of available processor cores, in parallel. Since actors do not share state,[1] you do not have to worry about data races even if you don't know the actual execution order in advance. In fact, for best performance and scalability we would like to have as many actors as possible executed in parallel!

However, in some cases it can be helpful to execute actors deterministically. The main reason is that a deterministic execution enables reproducing program executions that are not influenced by timing-dependent variations in thread scheduling, which make multi-threaded programs extremely hard to test.

For example, consider a concurrent application simulating mechanical gears and motors. Assume that each gear's speed is adjusted using a controller. To model the real-world concurrency, we represent each gear and the controller as an actor. Listing 7.5 shows the implementation of a gear as an actor. The Gear actor responds to SyncGear messages that cause the gear

---

[1]Currently this is a mere convention; however, efforts exist to have actor isolation checked using an annotation checker plug-in for the Scala compiler.

91

```scala
case class SyncGear(s: Int)
case class SyncDone(g: Gear)

class Gear(val id: Int, var speed: Int, val controller: Actor)
    extends Actor {
  def act() {
    loop {
      react {
        case SyncGear(targetSpeed: Int) =>
          println("[Gear "+id+
                  "] synchronize from current speed " + speed +
                  " to target speed " + targetSpeed)
          adjustSpeedTo(targetSpeed)
      }
    }
  }

  def adjustSpeedTo(targetSpeed: Int) {
    if (targetSpeed > speed) {
      speed += 1
      self ! SyncGear(targetSpeed)
    } else if (targetSpeed < speed) {
      speed -= 1
      self ! SyncGear(targetSpeed)
    } else if (targetSpeed == speed) {
      println("[Gear " + id + "] has target speed")
      controller ! SyncDone(this)
      exit()
    }
  }
}
```

Listing 7.5 · Synchronizing the speed of Gear actors.

to adjust its speed in a step-wise manner. For instance, a gear with current speed 7 units requires two steps to adjust its speed to 5 units. A SyncGear message initiates each step. To process each message, the gear decrements its speed by a fixed amount and sends itself another SyncGear message if it has not reached its target speed. Otherwise, the gear reports to its controller that it has reached the target speed using a SyncDone message. Let's write a little driver to test the Gear actor:

```
object NonDeterministicGears {
  def main(args: Array[String]) {
    actor {
      val g1 = (new Gear(1, 7, self)).start()
      val g2 = (new Gear(2, 1, self)).start()
      g1 ! SyncGear(5)
      g2 ! SyncGear(5)
      react { case SyncDone(_) =>
        react { case SyncDone(_) => }
      }
    }
  }
}
```

The above driver creates two gears that, initially, are running at speeds 7 and 1, respectively. Afterward the controller actor instructs the gears to adjust their speed to 5 by sending asynchronous SyncGear messages. Finally, it waits until both gears have synchronized their speeds. Running the driver produces output such as the following:

```
[Gear 2] synchronize from current speed 1 to target speed 5
[Gear 2] synchronize from current speed 2 to target speed 5
[Gear 1] synchronize from current speed 7 to target speed 5
[Gear 1] synchronize from current speed 6 to target speed 5
[Gear 1] synchronize from current speed 5 to target speed 5
[Gear 2] synchronize from current speed 3 to target speed 5
[Gear 1] has target speed
[Gear 2] synchronize from current speed 4 to target speed 5
[Gear 2] synchronize from current speed 5 to target speed 5
[Gear 2] has target speed
```

93

As you can see, the speed-adjusting steps of the different gears are interleaved, since the gear actors are running concurrently. A subsequent program run may produce an entirely different interleaving of the steps. However, this means that you could not use the above driver for a unit test that compares the actual output to some expected output.

Using the `SingleThreadedScheduler` class (which resides in package `scala.actors.scheduler`), you can make the execution of concurrent actors deterministic. As its name suggests, this scheduler runs the behavior of all actors on a single thread. Since that thread's execution is deterministic, the entire actor system executes deterministically. In particular, any side effects that actors might have as part of their reaction to messages, such as I/O, is done in the same order in all program runs.

Usually, running actors on a single thread means that the reaction of an actor receiving a message is immediately executed on the same thread that has been executing that message's sender. Since it is a valid pattern to have an actor sending messages to itself in a loop, sometimes the scheduler must delay the processing of a message to avoid a stack overflow. For such situations, the scheduler maintains a queue of reactions that are executed when there is nothing else left to do. However, some reactions may remain in the scheduler's queue just before the application should terminate. Therefore, to make sure that the scheduler processes all tasks, you have to invoke `shutdown` explicitly.

7.2   Managed blocking

The actor runtime system uses a thread pool, which is initialized to use a relatively small number of worker threads. By default, the number of workers used is twice the number of processor cores available to the JVM. In many cases, this configuration allows executing actors with a maximum degree of parallelism while consuming only a few system resources for the thread pool. In particular, actor programs that use only event-based operations, such as `react`, can always be executed using a fixed number of worker threads.

However, in some cases, actors use a mix of event-based code and thread-based code. For instance, some methods like `receive` are implemented using thread-blocking operations. Moreover, actor-based code may have to interoperate with code using the Java's `java.util.concurrent` concurrency utilities. In both cases, operations that may block the underlying thread have

```
import scala.actors.Actor._
import java.util.concurrent.CountDownLatch

object PoolLockup {

  def main(args: Array[String]) {
    val numCores = Runtime.getRuntime().availableProcessors()
    println("available cores: " + numCores)

    val latch = new CountDownLatch(1)
    for (i <- 1 to (numCores * 2)) actor {
      latch.await()
      println("actor " + i + " done")
    }

    actor { latch.countDown() }
  }
}
```

Listing 7.6 · Blocked actors may lock up the thread pool.

to be used with care, so as to avoid locking up the entire thread pool.

For example, Listing 7.6 shows what happens if too many actors are blocked simultaneously. To simplify the demonstration, we use an instance of the CountDownLatch class in the java.util.concurrent package. Note that even though the actual code example may not be very useful in and of itself, there are probably places in your actor-based program where the Java concurrency utility classes come in handy. Therefore, the following discussion should be useful to anyone who wants to reuse blocking concurrency code in his or her actor code.

Basically, we use a CountDownLatch to notify a bunch of actors once the "main actor" reaches a certain point. To do this, we initialize the latch to one, and tell our actors to wait until the latch becomes zero. Once the main actor sets the latch to zero, the other actors can continue and print a message before terminating. Now, the problem is that if too many actors wait for the latch to become zero, all worker threads in the underlying thread pool may be blocked, so that there is no thread left to execute the main actor. As a result, the blocked actors wait indefinitely, the thread pool is locked up, and the program fails to terminate. Note that in the example we took care to start twice as many blocking actors as there are processor cores available to the JVM. This corresponds exactly to the number of pool threads created by default. Therefore, starting fewer blocking actors will not cause problems, since there will be a pool thread left to execute the main actor, which releases the blocked actors.

There are several ways to prevent the thread pool from locking up our actor-based program:

- Configuring the thread pool to create more worker threads on start up

- Using *managed blocking* to dynamically resize the thread pool before invoking a blocking operation

The first alternative can be implemented either by using the JVM properties `actors.corePoolSize` and `actors.maxPoolSize` (see Chapter 5), or by using a customized scheduler (see Section 7.1). However, pre-configuring the thread pool size can be fragile if the number of blocking actors is hard to predict. Moreover, overprovisioning of thread pool resources is likely to negatively impact your application's performance.

The second alternative is a much more efficient way of dealing with blocking operations, since the thread pool grows only on demand, and (usually) only for a short period of time. It also avoids the problem of having to predict the maximum number of actors that may be blocked simultaneously. The basic idea of managed blocking is to invoke blocking operations indirectly through an interface that allows the thread pool to resize itself before blocking. Additionally, the interface allows the pool to query a wrapped blocking operation to check whether it no longer needs to block. This enables shrinking the pool back to the size it had before growing to accommodate the blocking operation.

Listing 7.7 shows how you can use the `ManagedBlocker` interface to avoid locking up the thread pool. Managed blocking requires the use of methods that are not accessible when defining actors inline using `actor {` `... }`. Therefore, you have to create your blocking actors by subclassing the `Actor` trait. Note that inside the body of `act` we replaced the invocation of `latch.await()` with a call to `managedBlock`, a method declared in the `IScheduler` trait. It is invoked on the `scheduler` instance that is used to execute the current actor (`this`). `managedBlock` takes an instance of `ManagedBlocker` as an argument. You use the `ManagedBlocker` trait to

```scala
import scala.actors.Actor
import scala.actors.Actor._
import scala.concurrent.ManagedBlocker
import java.util.concurrent.CountDownLatch

object ManagedBlocking {

  class BlockingActor(i: Int, latch: CountDownLatch)
      extends Actor {
    val blocker = new ManagedBlocker {
      def block() = { latch.await(); true }
      def isReleasable = { latch.getCount == 0 }
    }
    def act() {
      scheduler.managedBlock(blocker)
      println("actor " + i + " done")
    }
  }

  def main(args: Array[String]) {
    val numCores = Runtime.getRuntime().availableProcessors()
    println("available cores: " + numCores)

    val latch = new CountDownLatch(1)
    for (i <- 1 to (numCores * 2))
      (new BlockingActor(i, latch)).start()

    actor { latch.countDown() }
  }
}
```

Listing 7.7 · Using managed blocking to prevent thread-pool lock up.

wrap blocking operations in a way that allows the underlying thread pool to choose when and how to invoke that operation. The trait contains the following two methods:

- def block(): Boolean

- def isReleasable: Boolean

The two methods are supposed to be implemented in the following way: The block method invokes a method that possibly blocks the current thread. The underlying thread pool makes sure to invoke block only in a context where blocking is safe; for instance, if there are no idle worker threads left, it first creates an additional thread that can process submitted tasks in the case all other workers are blocked. The Boolean result indicates whether the current thread might still have to block even after the invocation of block has returned. In most cases, it is sufficient to just return true, which indicates that no additional blocking is necessary. The isReleasable method, like block, indicates whether additional blocking is necessary. Unlike block, it should not invoke possibly blocking operations itself. Moreover, it can (and should) return true even if a previous invocation of block returned false, but blocking is no longer necessary.

The implementations of block and isReleasable in Listing 7.7 are straightforward. The block method simply invokes latch.await and returns true after that; clearly, once await has returned no additional blocking is necessary. In our implementation of isReleasable, we use the getCount method of CountDownLatch to determine whether the call to await has already unblocked the thread or not. Running the program extended with managed blocking in this way shows that the pool no longer locks up.

Managed blocking and receive

The receive method allows actors to receive messages in a thread-based way. This means that you can use receive just like any other possibly blocking operation. This is unlike the react method, which is more lightweight, but also more restricted. (Chapter 5 showed how to do event-based programming using react.) Since receive uses standard JVM monitors under the hood, it has the same potential problems as any other blocking code when invoked from within actors. However, since all variants of receive are implemented in objects and types in the scala.actors package, it uses managed blocking internally to avoid thread pool lock-ups. Consequently, there is no need to wrap invocations of `receive` in `ManagedBlockers` in user code.

Chapter 8

Remote Actors

Scala actors can communicate with each other not only within the same JVM address space, but also across virtual machines, and even across network nodes. To explain the constructs involved in using remote actors, in this chapter we will revisit the chat example application of Chapter 4. You will learn how to create remote actors, and how to address and communicate between remote actors.

The chat application of Chapter 4 creates an actor that is responsible for managing a chat room. Clients send various types of messages to the chat room actor, such as `Subscribe` and `Unsubscribe` messages. By making the chat room actor remotely accessible, the chat service can be used across a network.

8.1   Creating remote actors

Listing 8.1 shows how to turn the chat room actor into a remote actor. First, the actor runtime system needs to be informed that the actor wants to engage in remote communication with other actors. You do this by invoking the `alive` method of the `RemoteActor` object. It requires specifying a port number that is used to listen for incoming Transmission Control Protocol (TCP) connections. Actors running on different machines in the network use this port number to obtain a remote reference to the chat room actor.

The port number is not enough to uniquely identify the actor, however; several remote actors may be accessible via the same port. Therefore, remote actors must be registered under a name that is unique for a given port number by using the `register` method of `RemoteActor`:

```scala
import scala.actors.Actor
import Actor._
import scala.actors.remote.RemoteActor.{alive, register}

class ChatRoom extends Actor {
  def act() {
    alive(9000)
    register('chatroom, self)
    loop {
      receive {
        case Subscribe(user) =>       // handle subscriptions
        case Unsubscribe(user) =>     // handle unsubscriptions
        case UserPost(user, post) =>  // handle user posts
      }
    }
  }
}
```

Listing 8.1 · Making the chat room actor remotely accessible.

```scala
def register(name: Symbol, a: Actor): Unit
```

The method expects two arguments: The first argument is the name under which the actor should be registered. The second argument is the actor that should be registered; in the example in Listing 8.1, it is simply self. Subsequently, you can obtain a remote reference to the chat room actor using the port number, the IP address of the machine on which the actor is running, and the name under which it is registered on that machine.

Note that you can change the name under which an actor is registered by repeatedly invoking register, passing different symbols. However, at any point in time an actor is registered under a single name only. The most recent invocation of register "wins."

Messages for remote communication

To communicate with the chat room, messages must be serialized and sent over the network. Therefore, the message classes need to be serializable. Fortunately, the message classes defined in Listing 4.1 are all case classes, which are serializable by default.

8.2   Remote communication

The chat room actor can now receive messages from actors running on different nodes on the network. However, its clients first have to obtain a remote reference to it. You can obtain such a reference using the `select` method of the `RemoteActor` object:

```
def select(node: Node, sym: Symbol): AbstractActor
```

The first argument is a `Node` instance that specifies the IP address and port number of the target node. The second argument is the target actor's name. Invoking `select` returns an object of type `AbstractActor`. You can think of `AbstractActor` as a trait that contains all the functionality of `Actor` except for methods that are not supported by remote actors, such as `start`, `restart`, and `getState`.

Node is a case class defined as follows:

```
case class Node(address: String, port: Int)
```

For example, let's select the chat room actor running on the local node on port 9000:

```
val chatRoom = select(Node("127.0.0.1", 9000), 'chatroom)
```

You can then use the `AbstractActor` reference that `select` returns to communicate with the chat room using the usual message send operations:

```
chatRoom ! Subscribe(User("Alice"))
chatRoom !? Subscribe(User("Bob"))
val future = chatRoom !! Subscribe(User("Charly"))
...
```

Just like with local actors, in all the above cases the remote actor implicitly receives a reference to the sending actor. As before, the remote actor can access the reference via the `sender` method of the `Actor` object. This means that the chat room actor's code to process incoming messages does not have to change.

Selecting an actor using a name that has no actor registered on the target node will *not* cause the `select` invocation to fail (by throwing an exception, say). Instead, the `AbstractActor` reference returned by `select` is *lazy* (or *delayed*) in the sense that no attempt to communicate with the remote node is made at that point. The `select` method merely creates a proxy object that forwards all messages it receives to the remote actor. Sending a message to a remote actor (or rather, its proxy) will result in a lost message if the symbol passed to `select` is not registered with an existing actor on the target node.

Linking to remote actors   An actor can link itself to a remote actor just like a local actor. It does not matter whether the receiver of a `link` invocation is local or remote. Reacting to the termination of linked remote actors is unchanged compared to the non-remote case, as discussed in Chapter 6.

8.3   A remote start service

In a distributed application, it is often useful to have a parent actor manage several child actors that run on different nodes on the network. Moreover, the number of child actors usually is not fixed when the application (or the parent actor) starts; instead, the parent actor must be able to start child actors dynamically (depending on input data, the state of the application, and so forth). This design typically requires a service that allows you to start actors remotely. Using such a remote start service, a parent actor can start new child actors on nodes different from its own node. In this section, we will explain how to implement such a remote start service.

We can model our remote start service as a remote actor that responds to the following two types of messages:

```
case class Start(clazz: Class[_ <: Actor])
case object Stop
```

An instance of the `Start` case class should instruct the remote start service to create and start an actor of the type specified by the `clazz` argument. Instances of type `Class[_ <: Actor]` are runtime representations of classes that extend the `Actor` trait. In general, we can use an object of type `Class[A]` to create instances of class A.[1] This means that we can use the argument of a `Start` message to create `Actor` instances, which we can then start on the remote node. The `Stop` case object is a message instructing the remote start service to terminate itself.

---

[1]Java's reflection framework adds the constraint that the instantiated class type must define a no-argument constructor.

```
class Server extends Actor {
  var numStarted = 0
  def act() {
    alive(19000)
    register('server, this)
    println("remote start server running...")
    loop {
      react {
        case Start(clazz) =>
          val a: Actor = clazz.newInstance()
          a.start()
          numStarted += 1
          reply()
        case Stop =>
          println("remote start server started " +
                  numStarted + " remote actors")
          exit()
      }
    }
  }
}
```

Listing 8.2 · A server actor implementing a remote start service.

Listing 8.2 shows a Server actor that implements a basic remote start service. Inside the act method we use alive and register to make the actor remotely accessible on port 19000 under the name 'server. After that the actor loops, reacting to the above Start and Stop messages. When the next message matches the Start(clazz) pattern, we create a new instance of the Actor subclass that clazz represents by invoking newInstance. The object returned by newInstance has type Actor since the type parameter in the clazz type is constrained to be an Actor subtype. After starting the new actor, the remote start actor replies to the sender of the Start message; this is because Start messages are supposed to be sent synchronously, which ensures that the new actor has been started when the synchronous message send completes.

Listing 8.3 shows an EchoActor class that is suitable for remote starting.

```
class EchoActor extends Actor {
  def act() {
    alive(19000)
    register('echo, this)
    react {
      case any => reply("echo: " + any)
    }
  }
}
```

Listing 8.3 · An echo actor that you can start remotely.

To be able to interact with new EchoActor instances remotely, we use the alive and register methods as in previous examples. Note that calling alive twice on the same node with the same port number argument has no effect. This is important, since the alive invocation of a new EchoActor instance will be called while running on the same node as the Server actor. Let's use our remote start service to start a new EchoActor:

```
val server = select(Node("localhost", 19000), 'server)
server !? Start(classOf[EchoActor])
val echo = select(Node("localhost", 19000), 'echo)
val resp = echo !? "hello"
println("remote start client received " + resp)
```

First, we obtain the server remote reference to the remote start service using select. To start a new instance of EchoActor on the node that runs the remote start service, we send a Start(classOf[EchoActor]) message to the server. Then we can reference the remotely started actor using select with the name that the EchoActor used to register itself on the remote node. The echo reference is a normal remote actor reference; as expected, running the above code results in the following message printed to the console:

```
remote start client received echo: hello
```

Chapter 9

Distributed and Parallel Computing

The Scala Actors API puts a powerful, yet simple, parallel computing framework built on top of the JVM at your disposal. This chapter illustrates how to accomplish some common parallel and distributed computing tasks with actors. In particular, we focus on two patterns that are useful in many applications: MAPREDUCE and reliable broadcasting. MAPREDUCE is a paradigm for parallel and distributed programming that has been established as a de facto standard to accomplish a wide variety of tasks, such as hypertext document processing, machine learning, and data mining. Reliable broadcasting, on the other hand, is often necessary in distributed applications where machines in a cluster can fail due to hardware outages or communication delays.

9.1 MapReduce

MAPREDUCE is a parallel computing framework originally developed at Google to simplify programming large-scale distributed computations while providing fault tolerance and excellent scalability.[1] MAPREDUCE simplifies parallel programming, since the programmer does not have to manage parallelism explicitly. Instead, the MAPREDUCE framework takes care of creating parallel tasks, synchronizing them, and distributing the workload. Moreover, a MAPREDUCE implementation also typically provides fault tolerance. This means that you can successfully complete a MAPREDUCE computation even if some machines in the cluster fail to compute or communicate their results.

---

[1] Dean and Ghemawat, "MapReduce: Simplified Data Processing on Large Clusters" [Dea08]

MapReduce history Why was MAPREDUCE invented at Google? Jeffrey Dean and Sanjay Ghemawat, the Google engineers that invented MAPRE-DUCE, recount that the abstraction emerged after they had written hundreds of special-purpose computations to process large amounts of raw data, such as crawled web pages, web server logs, *etc.* While the computations performed on the data were simple, the input data was so large that the computation had to be performed in parallel if it was to finish within a reasonable amount of time.

Google's data centers do not consist of expensive supercomputers. Instead, they are populated with large clusters of inexpensive commodity hardware; typically, Linux desktop machines connected via an ethernet network. Computations thus needed to be parallelized for a distributed environment in which network bandwidth is scarce and machine failures are common.

As a result, the simplicity of the computations was lost in the complexity of recurring issues, such as how to distribute the data, how to parallelize the computation across machines, how to deal with load imbalance, machine failures, and so on. Inspired by the *map* and *reduce* higher-order functions from functional programming, Dean and Ghemawat identified a way to separate the computation-specific parts into higher-order functions. The programmer supplies just these functions, and the MAPREDUCE framework calls them on an appropriate machine with part of the input data, hiding most of the complexity of the parallel and distributed computing environment. MAPREDUCE truly is a success story based on the principles of higher-order functional programming.

Let's look at a concrete example that is amenable to parallel processing. Consider the task of building an inverted index for a collection of text files. You can use an inverted index to quickly look up the files in which a given word occurs. To create such an index, you must "invert" the mapping from files to their contents (hence, the name "inverted index"). Our strategy for building it is as follows: For each file f, we will create a list that contains pairs, (word, f), where word is a word occurring in f. This means that each of these lists contains pairs that all have the same second component—the file in which the word occurs. In the next step, we will go through all of the lists, and fill a Map that maps words to lists of files in which they occur; the file lists should not contain duplicates. The reason why we first create lists of word/file pairs (instead of directly building the Map) is that this allows us to parallelize the task; each file can be processed in parallel to create the intermediate lists.

```
def invertedIndex(input: List[(File, List[String])]) = {
  val master = self
  val workers = for ((file, words) <- input) yield
    actor {
      val wordsAndFiles = for (word <- words) yield (word, file)
      master ! Intermediate(wordsAndFiles)
    }
  var intermediates = List[(String, File)]()
  for (_ <- 1 to input.length)
    receive {
      case Intermediate(list) => intermediates :::= list
    }
  var dict = Map[String, List[File]]() withDefault (k => List())
  for ((word, file) <- intermediates)
    dict += (word -> (file :: dict(word)))
  var result = Map[String, List[File]]()
  for ((word, files) <- dict)
    result += (word -> files.distinct)
  result
}
```

Listing 9.1 · A function for building an inverted index.

Listing 9.1 shows a parallel implementation using actors. For each file in the input list, we create a worker actor. A worker generates the list of word/file pairs, and sends them in an Intermediate message back to the master actor (master is the actor invoking the invertedIndex method). The Intermediate class is defined as follows:

```
case class Intermediate(list: List[(String, File)])
```

The master actor concatenates all the intermediate results it receives that yield a list of type List[(String, File)]. The word/file pairs in this list are inserted into a Map, so that each word maps to a list of files in which it occurs. Finally, we remove duplicates from these file lists, yielding the result map that represents our inverted index (the inferred result type of the invertedIndex method is Map[String, List[File]]).

The parallel construction of our inverted index follows a certain pattern that, as it turns out, is useful for many applications. Let's walk through that pattern step-by-step. In the first step, a function—let's call it the mapping function—is applied to each pair in the input list in order to produce another list of pairs.

In the example, we generate for each input pair of type (File, List[String]) a list of pairs of type (String, File)—each pair associates a word with the file in which it occurs. We can encapsulate just this computation in the following function:

```
def mapIndex(file: File, words: List[String]) =
  for (word <- words) yield (word, file)
```

(The inferred result type of mapIndex is List[(String, File)]). You can apply the mapping function (mapIndex or some other function) in parallel by creating a worker actor for each input pair:

```
val workers = for ((key, value) <- input) yield
  actor {
    master ! Intermediate(mapping(key, value))
  }
```

Note that we changed the code to call the generic mapping function to produce the list of intermediate pairs. Moreover, we renamed the components of an input pair, replacing (file, words) with (key, value). The reason is that besides factoring out the mapping function, this "mapping stage" can be generalized further to operate on arbitrary inputs of type List[(K, V)]. The type of the intermediate output pairs can be generic, too. Instead of always producing a List[(String, File)], a mapping function may produce a List[(K2, V2)]. Taken together, the generic mapping function has type (K, V) => List[(K2, V2)].

The next step is to collect the intermediate results sent to the master actor in Intermediate messages:

```
var intermediates = List[(K2, V2)]()
for (_ <- 1 to input.length)
  receive {
    case Intermediate(list) => intermediates :::= list
  }
```

110

After we apply the `mapping` function to each input pair (a file paired with its contents), we group the intermediate output pairs by their first component, inserting them into a `Map`:

```
var dict = Map[K2, List[V2]]() withDefault (k => List())
for ((key, value) <- intermediates)
  dict += (key -> (value :: dict(key)))
```

Subsequently, the intermediate results that have been grouped by their key are further processed using a function—let's call it the `reducing` function—to yield the final result.

In the example, the list of files corresponding to each word is reduced by removing duplicates. Again, it is easy to define a function that encapsulates just this reduction step:

```
def reduceIndex(key: String, files: List[File]) =
  files.distinct
```

The `reducing` function is applied to each entry in the `dict` map of intermediate results, yielding the `result` map:

```
var result = Map[K2, List[V2]]()
for ((key, value) <- dict)
  result += (key -> reducing(key, value))
```

According to its use in the above reduction step, the `reducing` function has type `(K2, List[V2]) => List[V2]`.

Listing 9.2 shows a generic function, called `mapReduce`, that implements the parallel programming pattern that we just described. As its name suggests, it is a basic (in-memory) MAPREDUCE implementation.

Note that we have moved the declaration of the `Intermediate` case class into the method body. The reason is that this allows us to recover more type information when pattern matching on `Intermediate` messages. Let's see what happens if `Intermediate` is defined outside the `mapReduceBasic` method, like this:

```
case class Intermediate[K2, V2](list: List[(K2, V2)])
```

Now, when pattern matching against an `Intermediate` instance, an instantiation of the type parameters has to be found. When matching against

111

```
def mapReduceBasic[K, V, K2, V2](
  input: List[(K, V)],
  mapping: (K, V) => List[(K2, V2)],
  reducing: (K2, List[V2]) => List[V2]
): Map[K2, List[V2]] = {
  case class Intermediate(list: List[(K2, V2)])

  val master = self
  val workers = for ((key, value) <- input) yield
    actor {
      master ! Intermediate(mapping(key, value))
    }

  var intermediates = List[(K2, V2)]()
  for (_ <- 1 to input.length)
    receive {
      case Intermediate(list) => intermediates :::= list
    }

  var dict = Map[K2, List[V2]]() withDefault (k => List())
  for ((key, value) <- intermediates)
    dict += (key -> (value :: dict(key)))

  var result = Map[K2, List[V2]]()
  for ((key, value) <- dict)
    result += (key -> reducing(key, value))
  result
}
```

Listing 9.2 · A basic MAPREDUCE implementation.

Intermediate messages received inside `mapReduceBasic`, K2 and V2 are both instantiated to Any. As a result, we get the following type error:

```
...: error: type mismatch;
 found   : List[(Any, Any)]
 required: List[(K2, V2)]
         case Intermediate(list) => intermediates :::= list
                                                          ^
```

```
one error found
```

By moving the definition of the `Intermediate` class into the method body, the type of its `list` argument is `List[(K2, V2)]`, where K2 and V2 are no longer generic, but fixed to the type arguments of the enclosing method. Then, in the pattern match, `list` has type `List[(K2, V2)]`, which makes it compatible with the type of the `intermediates` list.

Parallel reductions   We can improve the basic MAPREDUCE implementation shown above by parallelizing the reduction stage in addition to the mapping stage. Listing 9.3 shows how to modify our previous implementation to apply the `reducing` function in parallel. Similar to the mapping stage, we create an actor for each key in the `dict` map. The actor applies the `reducing` function to the key and the values with which the key is associated in `dict`. The result is sent to the `master` actor in a message of type `Reduced`. The `master` collects these messages like the `Intermediate` messages before; this time yielding the final `result` map.

Now that we have parallelized the reduction stage, we'll summarize the basic execution model of MAPREDUCE:

- The MAPREDUCE computation is supervised by a single actor, called the *master*.

- Input data is represented as a list of "records," represented here as pairs of type (K, V). The master partitions the input data across a set of "mapper" workers.

- Each mapper worker is a separate actor that applies the `mapping` function to a different part of the input data in parallel. For each input pair (k, v), a mapper generates a new list of pairs, which may be of a different type (K2, V2).

113

```
def mapReduce[K, V, K2, V2](
  input: List[(K, V)],
  mapping: (K, V) => List[(K2, V2)],
  reducing: (K2, List[V2]) => List[V2]
): Map[K2, List[V2]] = {
  case class Intermediate(list: List[(K2, V2)])
  case class Reduced(key: K2, values: List[V2])

  // ...

  val reducers = for ((key, values) <- dict) yield
    actor {
      master ! Reduced(key, reducing(key, values))
    }

  var result = Map[K2, List[V2]]()
  for (_ <- 1 to dict.size)
    receive {
      case Reduced(key, values) =>
        result += (key -> values)
    }

  result
}
```

Listing 9.3 · Applying the reducing function in parallel.

- The master collects the intermediate results of the mapping stage and then sorts this data according to the intermediate key type K2.

- For each such key, the master asks a "reducer" worker to reduce the list of values of type V2. Again, each reducer is a separate actor that can perform this step in parallel. Reducers may return a List[V2], but it is not uncommon for this list to contain a single, reduced value.

- The master collects the reduced V2 values and simply combines them in a result Map.

Figure 9.1 illustrates the flow of data between master, mapper, and reducer actors for the inverted index example.

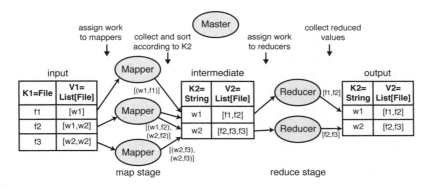

Figure 9.1 · Data flow in a basic MAPREDUCE implementation.

Fault-tolerance Our basic implementation of MAPREDUCE is not fault-tolerant; that is, it cannot tolerate the failures of either the master actor or any of the mapper or reducer worker actors. If a worker crashes, the master will block waiting for a reply indefinitely.

In our example implementation, since we are assuming a shared-memory environment, chances are that a system failure will bring all of the actors to a halt. However, in a distributed MAPREDUCE implementation, the master and workers execute on different machines. In such an environment, partial failure, for example, a single machine failure, can be common. Therefore, let us extend our sample implementation to at least tolerate worker failures.

We will use the mechanisms described in Section 6.2 to implement fault tolerance: The master actor will link itself to all of the workers it spawns, and is configured to trap exits (using `self.trapExit = true`). This causes the worker actors to send a special `Exit` message to the master when they terminate, allowing the master to identify crashed workers.

Listing 9.4 extends the basic MAPREDUCE implementation shown in Listing 9.2 with this fault-tolerance mechanism. Notice that the mapper actors are spawned using `link` instead of `actor` such that they are automatically linked to the master actor.

For each spawned worker, the master also keeps track of what key-value pair it assigned to that worker. When a worker terminates with an abnormal reason, the master looks up what pair it assigned to the terminated worker and spawns a new worker to process the same input. When a worker terminates with a `'normal` reason, the master decrements a count identifying the

115

```
def mapreduce[K, V, K2, V2](
  input: List[(K, V)],
  mapping: (K, V) => List[(K2, V2)],
  reducing: (K2, List[V2]) => List[V2]
): Map[K2, List[V2]] = {
  case class Intermediate(list: List[(K2, V2)])
  case class Reduced(key: K2, values: List[V2])

  val master = self
  self.trapExit = true
  var assignedMappers = Map[Actor, (K, V)]()

  def spawnMapper(key: K, value: V) = {
    val mapper = link {
      master ! Intermediate(mapping(key, value))
    }
    assignedMappers += (mapper -> (key, value))
    mapper
  }

  for ((key, value) <- input)
    spawnMapper(key, value)

  var intermediates = List[(K2, V2)]()
  var nleft = input.length
  while (nleft > 0)
    receive {
      case Intermediate(list) => intermediates :::= list
      case Exit(from, 'normal) => nleft -= 1
      case Exit(from, reason) =>
        // retrieve assigned work
        val (key, value) = assignedMappers(from)
        // spawn new worker to re-execute the work
        spawnMapper(key, value)
    }
  // ...
```

Listing 9.4 · A MAPREDUCE implementation that tolerates mapper faults.

number of outstanding jobs. When that number becomes zero, the master knows that all workers (either the original or restarted ones) have finished.

Our technique of simply re-executing a failed mapping is sound as long as the mapping function is really a function; that is, if it has no side effects. Otherwise, failures may affect the outcome of a MAPREDUCE computation. As Scala provides the right building blocks to program in a functional style, restricting yourself to a purely functional subset to implement the mapping and reducing functions is usually not a problem.

Another point worth mentioning is that this simple re-execution strategy does not cope with deterministic errors. Say, for example, that there is a bug in the mapping function that only manifests itself for particular values of type K. The bug may cause an exception, terminating the worker. In this case, simply starting a new worker to process the same input will cause the exception again, leading to endless re-execution and no progress for the master. Actual MAPREDUCE implementations deal with such cases by skipping over such "bad" input data, giving up after a few retries. This makes sense, since MAPREDUCE is typically used for workloads where the loss of a little input data can still lead to a useful answer (for example, indexing, search, data mining, and so on).

Note that even in this extended implementation, the master is still a single point of failure: If it crashes, the entire MAPREDUCE computation is brought to a halt. If the chance of a master failure is small and the MAPREDUCE computation is not too large, it may not be worth dealing with this case. Otherwise, you have to either replicate the master, or periodically checkpoint the state of the master to persistent storage, but these techniques are beyond what we can address in this chapter.

Coarse-grained worker tasks   In our previous MAPREDUCE implementations, a new mapper actor is spawned for each input key K and a new reducer actor is spawned for each intermediate key K2. When the input data is large (for example, when indexing thousands of files, each containing thousands of words), this simple strategy may introduce too much overhead. To reduce this overhead, we can make the tasks assigned to the mapper and reducer workers more coarse-grained by having each of them process multiple key-value pairs.

Listing 9.5 builds on the MAPREDUCE implementation from Listing 9.3 and adds support for coarse-grained tasks. The coarse-grained implementation takes two extra arguments: numMappers, the number of parallel mapper workers to spawn; and numReducers, the number of parallel reducer workers to spawn.

The magic of this implementation is hidden inside a useful function from the Scala Seq API: grouped. Calling grouped(n) on a sequence returns a new sequence, which returns elements from the original sequence that are grouped in groups of size n. To create more coarse-grained tasks, we split the input and the intermediate data into groups of an appropriate size, and then spawn a worker actor per group. Each such worker processes all key-value pairs in its assigned group.

To ensure that we spawn only numMappers mappers, it suffices to group the input data into groups of size input.length / numMappers. For example, if numMappers is 10 and we need to process 5000 files, then each mapper will need to process 500 pairs. Similarly, we partition the dictionary dict containing the sorted intermediate data into groups of size dict.size / numReducers. If the size of the data is not exactly divisible by the required number of workers, the last group returned by grouped will contain fewer elements, so the last worker will get assigned less work.

Our simple strategy of dividing work equally among the workers is fine as long as the amount of processing to be done is approximately the same for all keys. Actual MAPREDUCE implementations will often employ more elaborate data distribution techniques to balance the load between the workers at runtime if the work is not evenly distributed.

9.2   Reliable broadcast

When building a distributed application, it is often necessary that more than two actors operate in a coordinated manner. For example, you may want to ensure that all or none of your remote actors carry out some action while providing a way to handle the error case. If a set of remote actors should save their internal state to a database, for instance, then typically you want all or none of them to do it so that there is always a consistent view persisted to the database.

Basic broadcasting

You can instruct a number of actors to carry out some action by *broadcasting* a message to these actors. Listing 9.6 shows a simple broadcast implementa-

```scala
def coarseMapReduce[K, V, K2, V2](
  input: List[(K, V)],
  mapping: (K, V) => List[(K2, V2)],
  reducing: (K2, List[V2]) => List[V2],
  numMappers: Int, numReducers: Int): Map[K2, List[V2]] = {
  case class Intermediate(list: List[(K2, V2)])
  case class Reduced(key: K2, values: List[V2])

  val master = self
  for (group <- input.grouped(input.length / numMappers))
    actor {
      for ((key, value) <- group)
        master ! Intermediate(mapping(key, value))
    }
  var intermediates = ...

  var dict = Map[K2, List[V2]]() withDefault (k => List())
  for ((key, value) <- intermediates)
    dict += (key -> (value :: dict(key)))
  for (group <- dict.grouped(dict.size / numReducers))
    actor {
      for ((key, values) <- group)
        master ! Reduced(key, reducing(key, values))
    }

  var result = Map[K2, List[V2]]()
  for (_ <- 1 to dict.size)
    receive {
      case Reduced(key, values) =>
        result += (key -> values)
    }
  result
}
```

Listing 9.5 · MAPREDUCE with coarse-grained worker tasks.

```scala
abstract class BroadcastActor extends Actor {
  // can be set by external actor, therefore @volatile
  @volatile var isBroken = false
  private var canRun = true
  private var counter = 0L

  protected def broadcast(m: BSend) = if (!isBroken) {
    for (a <- m.recipients) a ! BDeliver(m.data)
  } else if (canRun) {
    canRun = false // simulate it being broken
    for (a <- m.recipients.take(2)) a ! BDeliver(m.data)
    println("error at " + this)
  }

  // to be overridden in subtraits
  protected def reaction: PartialFunction[Any, Unit] = {
    case BCast(msg, recipients) =>
      counter += 1
      broadcast(BSend(msg, recipients, counter))
    case 'stop =>
      exit()
  }

  def act = loopWhile (canRun) { react(reaction) }
}
```

Listing 9.6 · Best-effort broadcasting.

tion. First, we define a BroadcastActor that implements act in a way that allows the actor to react to messages of type BCast and the special 'stop message, which causes the actor to terminate. The BCast case class is defined as follows:

```scala
case class BCast(data: Any, recipients: Set[Actor])
```

A BCast message tells the actor to send some data to a set of actors specified in the message. Note how the message handlers are defined using the reaction member, which is a partial function that is passed to react inside the act method. This has the advantage that subclasses can override reaction to handle additional message patterns while inheriting some of the message handling logic from the super-trait. The broadcast method implements the actual message sending. broadcast is invoked passing a BSend message that contains the data, the set of recipients, and a time stamp (initially, we will not use the time stamp, though):

```
case class BSend(data: Any, recipients: Set[Actor],
      timestamp: Long)
```

To make things more interesting, we allow an actor to be "broken," which is expressed using the volatile isBroken field (the field is volatile to safely allow changing its value from a different actor). A broken broadcast actor fails to send the message to all of the recipients. The actual data is wrapped in a message of type BDeliver, which is defined as follows:

```
case class BDeliver(data: Any)
```

A BDeliver message indicates to the recipient that the data was delivered using a broadcast.

```
class MyActor extends BroadcastActor {
  override def reaction = super.reaction orElse {
    case BDeliver(data) =>
      println("Received broadcast message: " +
            data + " at " + this)
  }
}
```

Listing 9.7 · Using the broadcast implementation in user code.

To use the broadcast implementation in actual user code, we extend the BroadcastActor and override its reaction member, as shown in Listing 9.7. The message handling logic of BroadcastActor must be enabled alongside the new handler for BDeliver messages. To do this, we combine super.reaction with the new handler using orElse. As a result, MyActor instances respond to Broadcast and 'stop messages, as defined in BroadcastActor, in addition to BDeliver messages.

Let's try out this basic broadcast implementation:

```
val a1 = new MyActor; a1.start()
val a2 = new MyActor; a2.start()
```

```
val a3 = new MyActor; a3.start()
val a4 = new MyActor; a4.start()
a1 ! Broadcast("Hello!", Set(a1, a2, a3, a4))
```

As expected, running the above code will produce output like the following:

```
Received broadcast message: Hello! at MyActor@3c3c9217
Received broadcast message: Hello! at MyActor@15af33d6
Received broadcast message: Hello! at MyActor@54520eb
Received broadcast message: Hello! at MyActor@2c9b42e6
```

However, let's try and set actor a1's isBroken field to true and initiate another broadcast:

```
a1.isBroken = true
a1 ! Broadcast("Hello again!", Set(a1, a2, a3, a4))
```

Then, the output will look differently:

```
error at MyActor@15af33d6
Received broadcast message: Hello again! at MyActor@2c9b42e6
```

In the above run, only one other actor besides a1 itself received the "Hello again!" message, because a1 failed before sending out more messages. In an actual distributed application, the reason could be a machine failure or a network link that is down. To guarantee that all or no recipients receive the broadcast message, it is necessary to implement a *reliable broadcast*.

Reliable broadcasting

To make the message broadcasting reliable, we will extend our code to implement an algorithm known as *eager reliable broadcast*. The idea of this algorithm is that every recipient of a broadcast message should forward that message to every other recipient. Since the forwarding should be done regardless of any failure, broadcasting is *eager*.

We'll extend BroadcastActor as shown in Listing 9.8. An RbActor keeps track of the BSend messages that it has received using the delivered set. When it receives a BSend, the actor checks whether it has already processed that message by testing the condition delivered.contains(m) is true (since after processing a BSend message, it is added to the delivered set). If the actor receives a fresh BSend message, it'll invoke broadcast to

```
class RbActor extends BroadcastActor {
  var delivered = Set[BSend]()
  override def reaction = super.reaction orElse {
    case m @ BSend(data, _, _) =>
      if (!delivered.contains(m)) {
        delivered += m
        broadcast(m)
        this ! BDeliver(data)
      }
  }
}
```

Listing 9.8 · A reliable broadcast actor.

```
protected def broadcast(m: BSend) = if (!isBroken) {
  for (a <- m.recipients) a ! m
} else if (canRun) {
  canRun = false // simulate it being broken
  for (a <- m.recipients.take(2)) a ! m
  println("error at " + this)
}
```

Listing 9.9 · Sending messages with time stamps.

send it to all recipient actors. Moreover, it'll send itself a BDeliver message, indicating that it received the data via a reliable broadcast.

It is crucial here that each BSend message contains a time stamp. The time stamp is set in the BroadcastActor. The time stamp lets us identify to which broadcast a particular BSend message belongs. The messages forwarded by each RbActor do not change that time stamp. This way, each actor knows when it has already received a broadcast message, in which case it does not forward it further. However, for the RbActor to work properly we need to slightly change the implementation of the BroadcastActor. Basically, it is no longer sufficient to send a BDeliver message inside the broadcast method. The reason is that the RbActor needs to receive BSend messages, since only those contain time stamps. Therefore, we have to change the broadcast method accordingly; this is shown in Listing 9.9.

123

As you can see, the BroadcastActor now simply sends the BSend messages to the recipients (a ! m), instead of sending a BDeliver message that only contains the data (a ! BDeliver(m.data)).

Having made these changes, let's re-run our client code. Before we can do that, however, we first have to change MyActor to extend RbActor instead of BroadcastActor:

```
class MyActor extends RbActor {
  override def reaction = super.reaction orElse {
    case BDeliver(data) =>
      println("Received broadcast message: " +
              data + " at " + this)
  }
}
```

Running our short test code from above (setting a1.isBroken to true) should now produce output like the following:

```
error at MyActor@28e70e30
Received broadcast message: Hello again! at MyActor@5954864a
Received broadcast message: Hello again! at MyActor@3c3c9217
Received broadcast message: Hello again! at MyActor@1ff82982
```

As you can see, even though actor a1 failed after sending the broadcast message to itself and actor a2, actors a3 and a4 also received the message. The reason is that a2 sent the BSend message it received from a1 to all of its recipients, which includes a3 and a4. In fact, we can prove mathematically that the strategy of eager reliable broadcast will deliver a message to all or no recipients, provided the network communication between actors is based on a reliable transport protocol, such as TCP, which Scala's remote actors use by default.

Chapter 10

Akka Actors

Akka is a new actor-based framework for Scala that aims to provide a comprehensive tool set for robust cloud computing. Its main inspirations are Erlang and Scala actors. However, compared to Scala actors it makes different design decisions in several places, based upon its main target application, middleware for clusters, and the cloud. This chapter introduces the essentials of Akka from a user's perspective. It also explains the main differences to Scala actors, from an operational point of view.

All code in this chapter is based on Akka 1.2 using the akka-actor and akka-remote modules. You can obtain the Akka 1.2 release either from the Akka project website at http://akka.io/, or as part of the *Typesafe Stack* at http://typesafe.com/stack.

10.1   Creating Akka actors

Creating an actor in Akka involves three steps:

1. To implement the actor's behavior, Akka's Actor trait must be sub-classed. This step is analogous to the way Scala actors are created.

2. To be able to refer to the newly created actor, you must obtain an ActorRef that points to the actor. An ActorRef is a handle that you use to communicate with an actor as well as to control an actor's life cycle. We will have much more to say about ActorRefs in the following sections.

3. You must start the actor by invoking the start method on the new
ActorRef. In Akka, most of the actor API is accessed through
ActorRefs, in particular, starting and stopping actors.

As an example, let's re-implement the actor chain of Chapter 5 (see Listing 5.1 on page 57) using Akka. We start by subclassing Akka's Actor trait
to define the behavior of actors in the chain. This is shown in Listing 10.1.

```scala
import akka.actor.{Actor, ActorRef, Channel}
import Actor._

class ChainActor(next: Option[ActorRef]) extends Actor {
  var from: Channel[Any] = _

  def receive = {
    case 'Die =>
      from = self.channel
      if (next.isEmpty) {
        from ! 'Ack
        self.stop()
      } else
        next.get ! 'Die
    case 'Ack =>
      self.stop()
      from ! 'Ack
  }
}
```

Listing 10.1 · A simple chain actor in Akka.

Compared to Listing 5.1 you'll notice several differences:

1. The next actor is referred to using an ActorRef (more precisely, an
Option[ActorRef]). In Akka, it is only safe to refer to an actor directly; *i.e.*, without using an ActorRef inside the definition of a class
or trait that extends the Actor trait. We will talk more about this in
Section 10.2, where we show what happens if you try to interact with
an actor without going through an ActorRef.

2. An Akka actor uses a global message handler to process incoming
messages. Instead of invoking react for each incoming message, you

implement the `receive` member, which defines globally how incoming messages should be processed. The `receive` method returns a partial function that is applied to each incoming message.

3. As mentioned before, a large part of the Akka actor API is only accessible through `ActorRefs`. In the example, the sender of the message that is currently being processed is obtained using the `channel` member of `self`; it should come as no surprise that `self` has type `ActorRef`.

For creating an actor chain, we can use the following recursive function:

```
def buildChain(size: Int, next: Option[ActorRef]): ActorRef = {
  val a = actorOf(new ChainActor(next))
  a.start()
  if (size > 1) buildChain(size - 1, Some(a))
  else a
}
```

The function builds a chain starting from the last actor. As mentioned before, to interact with a newly created actor we need to obtain an `ActorRef` that points to it. You accomplish this by using the `actorOf` method (imported from the `Actor` object). It takes the new actor instance as an argument and returns a new `ActorRef`.

> ## Scaladoc and `ActorRef`
>
> When browsing the Scaladoc page for `ActorRef`, you will notice that it does not contain most of the methods that you would normally invoke on an `ActorRef`. For example, it does not list methods, `!`, `forward`, or `reply`. The reason is that Akka provides both a Scala API and a Java API. When using the Scala API, an `ActorRef` is implicitly converted to a `ScalaActorRef`. The `ScalaActorRef` trait, in turn, defines all of the methods of the Scala API.

10.2 ActorRefs

Note that the new actor has to be instantiated inside the invocation of `actorOf`. This ensures that there is an `ActorRef` created to interact with the

127

actor. As a result, the following code is erroneous:

```
val chainActor = new ChainActor(next) // Error!
val ref = actorOf(chainActor)
```

Running this code produces an initialization exception at runtime:

```
akka.actor.ActorInitializationException: ActorRef for instance
of actor [examples.akka.ChainActor] is not in scope.
        You can not create an instance of an actor explicitly
using 'new MyActor'.
        You have to use one of the factory methods in the 'Actor'
object to create a new actor.
        Either use:
                'val actor = Actor.actorOf[MyActor]', or
                'val actor = Actor.actorOf(new MyActor(..))'
```

Runtime exceptions, such as the one above, help avoid some basic errors using actors and `ActorRef`s. However, they cannot completely prevent direct references to actors from being leaked. For example, the following code will not throw an exception, although it should clearly be illegal:

```
var leaked: ChainActor = null
val ref = actorOf({leaked = new ChainActor(next); leaked})
```

Thus, while the `Actor` object's factory methods perform some basic safety checks, you still need to be careful to access actors using only `ActorRef`s.

10.3   Inter-actor interaction, interactively

To complete the actor chain example, we'll define a master actor that builds and controls an actor chain. With these definitions, shown in Listing 10.2, we'll use the interpreter shell to create an actor chain:

```
scala> import akka.actor.Actor._
import akka.actor.Actor._

scala> val master = actorOf(new MasterActor(5))
AKKA_HOME is defined as [.../akka-actors-1.1.2], loading con
fig from [.../akka-actors-1.1.2/config/akka.conf].
master: akka.actor.ActorRef = Actor[MasterActor:0291...a5d2]
```

```scala
class MasterActor(n: Int) extends Actor {
  val first = buildChain(n, None)
  def buildChain(size: Int, next: Option[ActorRef]): ActorRef =
    ...
  def receive = {
    case 'Start =>
      first ! 'Die
    case 'Ack =>
      println("OK, all actors died")
      self.stop()
  }
}
```

Listing 10.2 · A master actor controlling an actor chain.

```scala
scala> master.start()
res0: akka.actor.ActorRef = Actor[MasterActor:0291d...4a5d2]

scala> master ! 'Start
OK, all actors died
```

As you can see, it is possible to interact with actors outside the body of an actor class, from regular Scala code. However, there is a subtle but important difference when sending messages from outside an actor: accessing the sender inside the receiving actor (using `self.channel`) will return a channel that throws an exception whenever you try to send a reply to it. In contrast, in Scala actors a message's sender is always defined. In the case where a message is sent from outside an actor, an actor proxy is created that provides a message queue to the sending thread. As a result, it is always possible to receive replies on the sending thread in Scala actors.

10.4 Message handling

As you saw in the previous section, an Akka actor processes messages using a global message handler. Typically, this message handler is defined once and does not change over the lifetime of its actor. However, in some cases an actor handles different messages depending on its current state.

For example, consider a data processing framework where a master actor controls the processing steps. Before processing starts, the master actor receives the data to be processed (alternatively, it could receive information on how to obtain the data from disk or the network). Data processing should stop when a user-specified termination condition is satisfied. Thus, the master actor's message handler should look as follows:

```
def receive = {
  case InitData(item) =>
    // add item to data set
  case StartProcessing(condition) =>
    // process data set until 'condition' is true
}
```

An InitData(item) message adds item to the data set that the master actor manages. A data item could be a vertex in a large graph (for example, the graph containing all pages of the Wikipedia; in this graph, vertices correspond to articles, whereas edges are used to express links between pages). It could also be an image or a large matrix. A StartProcessing(condition) message instructs the master to start with the actual processing; it stops when the condition predicate is satisfied.

To do the actual processing in parallel, we can create a set of worker actors that each process a part of the data set. After each worker completes one "iteration," it informs the master actor using a WorkerDone message. The master actor can then test whether the termination condition is satisfied. If not, it instructs the workers to perform another iteration. Note that this messaging protocol requires the master actor to respond additionally to WorkerDone messages. However, it can handle these messages only after data processing has started. Therefore, the master actor has to *change its message handler* after receiving a StartProcessing message. We can do this using the become control structure; become takes as an argument the new message handler, which should be used to process all subsequent messages. We can use it to express the master actor's messaging protocol as follows:

```
def receive = {
  case InitData(item) =>
    // add item to data set
  case StartProcessing(condition) =>
    // process data set until 'condition' is true
```

```
    // instruct workers to process their part of
    // the data set
    for (worker <- workers) {
      worker ! Process(part)
    }
    become {
      case WorkerDone =>
        // the worker that sent this message is done
        ...
    }
  }
```

After handling WorkerDone messages using the message handler, which is activated using become, the master actor must check whether the termination condition is satisfied. In this case, it should change its behavior to the state where more data can be added to the data set and processing can be restarted by sending a StartProcessing message. To do this, we can use become, passing the message handler returned by receive:

```
become {
  case WorkerDone =>
    // the worker that sent this message is done
    ...
    if (condition())
      become(receive)
}
```

Unhandled messages

The become control structure enables message handling to depend on the actor's state. You can use state-dependent message handling to implement stateful abstractions, such as the unbounded buffer shown in Listing 10.3.

Here, we use become to limit the set of handled message types depending on the state of the actor's mailbox. For example, the actor handles a Get message only after it has received a corresponding Put message. (Put messages are asynchronous, whereas Get messages are synchronous.)

Let's interact with this buffer using the consumer defined in Listing 10.4. Being familiar with the behavior of react, you might be surprised to find

```scala
case class Put(elem: Int)
case object Get
case object Stop
class SimpleBuffer extends Actor {
  def receive = {
    case Put(data) =>
      become {
        case Get =>
          self.reply(data)
          become(receive)
      }
    case Stop =>
      self.stop()
  }
}
```

Listing 10.3 · Using become to implement a simple unbounded buffer.

that this simple buffer *does not work!* Running the code of Listing 10.4 produces an UnhandledMessageException:

```
Some(5)
[ERROR]   [7/8/11 12:41 PM] [akka:event-driven:dispatcher:global-1]
  [LocalActorRef] Put(3) akka.actor.UnhandledMessageException: Actor
  Actor[examples.akka.SimpleBuffer:40...d2] does not handle [Put(3)]

[ERROR]   [7/8/11 12:41 PM] [akka:event-driven:dispatcher:global-4]
  [LocalActorRef] Get   akka.actor.UnhandledMessageException: Actor
  Actor[examples.akka.SimpleBuffer:40...d2] does not handle [Get]

[ERROR]   [7/8/11 12:41 PM] [akka:event-driven:dispatcher:global-2]
  [LocalActorRef] Start akka.actor.UnhandledMessageException: Actor
  Actor[examples.akka.SimpleBuffer:40...d2] does not handle [Get]
```

As you can see, the first synchronous send of the consumer's Get message is successful, resulting in the consumer printing Some(5). Note that at this point the buffer actor's mailbox already contains the Put(3) message that was sent even before the consumer started. As a result, after processing the Get message, we use the currently active message handler to also process the Put(3) message. This causes an UnhandledMessageException

132

```
class Consumer(buf: ActorRef) extends Actor {
  def receive = {
    case Start =>
      // blocks actor until response is received
      println(buf ? Get)
      println(buf ? Get)
      buf ! Stop
      self.stop()
  }
}
object SimpleBuffer {
  def main(args: Array[String]) {
    val buffer = actorOf(new SimpleBuffer)
    buffer.start()
    buffer ! Put(5)
    buffer ! Put(3)
    val consumer = actorOf(new Consumer(buffer))
    consumer.start()
    consumer ! Start
  }
}
```

Listing 10.4 · A consumer interacting with the buffer.

to be thrown, since the partial function passed to become does not define a pattern-matching case for Put messages.

In summary, Akka requires message handlers to handle *all message types* that are possibly sent to the actor.[1] This means that it is impossible to let an actor's mailbox grow out of bounds, queueing messages that the actor will never handle. (This message reception semantics is a key difference between Akka's actors and Erlang/Scala actors.) On the other hand, it also means that implementing stateful actors requires slightly more work.

To make our buffer example work, we always have to handle both Put *and* Get messages, as shown in Listing 10.5. For handling Put messages when no corresponding Get message has been received, we use a queue

---

[1]More precisely, the isDefinedAt method of PartialFunction instances used as message handlers must return true for all messages the actor could receive.

```
class FlatBuffer extends Actor {
  var elems = Queue[Int]()
  var consumers = Queue[Channel[Any]]()
  def receive = {
    case Put(data) =>
      if (consumers.isEmpty) {
        elems = elems enqueue data
      } else {
        val (from, rest) = consumers.dequeue
        consumers = rest
        from ! data
      }
    case Get =>
      if (elems.isEmpty) {
        consumers = consumers enqueue self.channel
      } else {
        val (data, rest) = elems.dequeue
        elems = rest
        self.channel ! data
      }
    case Stop =>
      self.stop()
  }
}
```

Listing 10.5 · A buffer actor that handles both Put and Get messages.

(elems), which queues incoming data items. Consumers (actors that have sent a Get message) that are waiting to receive a data item are queued in another queue (consumers). Whenever an actor sends a Get message that cannot be handled, the actor is added to the consumers queue (more precisely, a channel pointing to the sending actor.) Otherwise, the buffer actor responds with a data item that is removed from the elems queue. Similarly, when consumers are waiting for a response, the buffer actor handles Put messages by removing the next consumer from the consumers queue, responding with the newly received data item.

10.5   Remote actors in Akka

Like the `scala.actors` package, Akka supports *remote actors*—actors that communicate over the network. In fact, Akka's remote actors may well be the main reason you are interested in Akka in the first place. They are feature-rich, powered by an efficient implementation based on Netty (for non-blocking network I/O), and support low-overhead message serialization, for example, using Google protocol buffers.[2]

To introduce Akka's remote actors step-by-step, we'll guide you through the creation of a remote "start" service similar to what you saw in Section 8.3. However, the following example is self-contained, so you don't have to read Section 8.3 if you haven't already done so.

Managing a cluster using actors

We will build a small cluster management service that allows a master node to start actors on other nodes in a cluster. Moreover, the cluster service should provide services to the remotely started actors, such as a list of references to cluster services on the neighboring nodes, graceful shutdown, *etc.*

The cluster service is centered around a *master service actor* that remotely communicates with a set of *cluster service actors*. The master actor manages all cluster service actors, broadcasts configuration information to them, and so forth. Each cluster service actor, in turn, manages the remote actors that are running on its local node. For example, to start a new remote actor on a particular node, the master actor sends a control message to the cluster service actor running on the target node; that cluster service actor then takes care of starting a new actor locally, and making it remotely accessible to the master actor.

To make things more concrete, let's look at some code. We'll begin with the master service, shown in Listing 10.6, which first starts when booting up the cluster service. The master service starts Akka's remote support by invoking `remote.start` (`remote` is a member of the `Actor` object), passing the host name and port of the master node. Then, we create a new `MasterService` actor (we'll discuss its implementation later), using `actorOf[MasterService]` (we also start the actor right away), and register it on the remote server of the current node, using `remote.register`. By reg-

---

[2]Google protocol buffers provide a language- and platform-neutral way to serialize data. See `http://code.google.com/apis/protocolbuffers/`.

```
import akka.actor.{Actor, ActorRef}
import Actor._
import java.util.concurrent.CountDownLatch
object MasterService {
  val doneInit = new CountDownLatch(1)
  private var _master: ActorRef = _

  def master: ActorRef = _master

  def main(args: Array[String]) {
    val hostname = args(0)
    val port = args(1).toInt
    val numNodes = args(2).toInt

    remote.start(hostname, port)

    _master = actorOf[MasterService].start()
    remote.register(_master)

    _master ? ClusterSize(numNodes)
    doneInit.await()
  }
}
```

Listing 10.6 · The MasterService object.

istering an actor in this way, we can obtain an ActorRef to that actor on any
node running Akka's remote support. (We'll use this functionality later for
communicating with the master actor from actors running on remote nodes.)
After that, we initialize the MasterService actor with the number of cluster nodes to be registered by sending it a message of type ClusterSize.
Note that message sends that use the ? operator are synchronous—they do
not return until the current actor has received a response. Finally, we use a
CountDownLatch to wait until the MasterService completes the initialization, which is the case when all cluster service actors have registered.

Listing 10.7 shows the code for MasterService actor. The master service waits for ClusterService actors to register using Announce messages.
Each message contains the host name and port number of the registering
cluster service. Upon receiving an Announce message, we obtain a remote
ActorRef, assigned to nodeRef, to the registering cluster service using one

of the `actorFor` methods of the `remote` object. We can use the returned ActorRef like any other (local) `ActorRef`. Next, we add to the nodeRefs map a mapping from the address (hostname and port) of the newly registered node to the nodeRef.

```scala
class MasterService extends Actor {
  var numNodes = 0
  var nodeRefs: Map[(String, Int), ActorRef] = Map()
  def receive = {
    case ClusterSize(numNodes) =>
      this.numNodes = numNodes
      println("[Master] waiting for " + numNodes +
              " nodes to register")
      self.reply()
    case Announce(newHost, newPort) =>
      println("[Master] new host " +
              newHost + ":" + newPort)
      val nodeRef = remote.actorFor(
        classOf[ClusterService].getCanonicalName,
        newHost,
        newPort)

      nodeRefs += ((newHost, newPort) -> nodeRef)

      if (nodeRefs.size == numNodes) {
        println("[Master] all nodes have registered")
        nodeRefs.values foreach { service =>
          service ? Nodes(nodeRefs.keys.toList)
        }
        MasterService.doneInit.countDown()
      }

      ...
  }
}
```

Listing 10.7 · The `MasterService` actor.

Finally, after the MasterService has received Announce messages from all cluster service actors (in which case, nodeRefs.size == numNodes), it broadcasts the network addresses of all nodes to the cluster service actors, and signals the end of its initialization by counting down the doneInit latch. This will unblock the main thread that has been executing the body of the MasterService object until the invocation of doneInit.await(), shown in Listing 10.6.

Listing 10.8 shows the ClusterService object. A cluster service instance starts similarly in a way to the master service: the main method of the ClusterService class's companion object sets up Akka's remote support and starts a ClusterService actor, passing it all the information needed to contact the master service.

Shutting down. The ClusterService actor's main thread handles termination using a CountDownLatch, which has an initial value of 1. When the ClusterService actor (which handles the actual communication with the master) determines that it should exit, it counts down the terminate latch. As a response to this, the main thread invokes registry.shutdownAll() to stop all actors that have been started on the local node, including the ClusterService actor.[3] Finally, it shuts down the remote service using remote.shutdown(). After that, the main thread of the cluster service node itself exits.

Listing 10.9 shows the ClusterService actor. It responds to several messages, but most interesting is what happens when a StartActorAt message is received. The MasterService uses this message to start an actor on a remote cluster service. This message contains an object of type Class[_ <: Actor], clazz, which is used to create a new Actor instance using actorOf. After registering the new actor on the remote service, the ClusterService actor sends it a message with the network addresses of all cluster nodes (remember that the master service broadcasts these addresses). Finally, it replies to the StartActorAt message to signal that the new actor is ready to receive remote messages.

To start an actor remotely via the StartActorAt message, we also need some functionality in the MasterService actor. One approach is to send StartActorAt messages to the master, in addition to the ClusterService,

---

[3]Akka registers all actors in a global actor registry, which you can access through the Actor object's registry member.

```
object ClusterService {
  val terminate = new CountDownLatch(1)

  def run(masterHostname: String,
          masterPort: Int,
          hostname: String,
          port: Int) {
    remote.start(hostname, port)

    val service = actorOf[ClusterService].start()
    remote.register(service)

    service ! Announce(masterHostname, masterPort)

    terminate.await()
    registry.shutdownAll() // also stops service actor
    remote.shutdown()
  }

  def main(args: Array[String]) {
    val masterHostname = args(0)
    val masterPort = args(1).toInt
    val hostname = args(2)
    val port = args(3).toInt
    run(masterHostname, masterPort, hostname, port)
  }
}
```

Listing 10.8 · The ClusterService object.

to instruct the master actor to forward a corresponding message to the target
ClusterService. You could do this by adding a pattern-matching case to
the MasterService actor's message handler:

```
case startMsg @ StartActorAt(host, port, clazz) =>
  nodeRefs((host, port)) ? startMsg
  val startedActor = remote.actorFor(
    clazz.getCanonicalName,
    host,
    port)
  self.reply(startedActor)
```

```scala
class ClusterService extends Actor {
  var allAddresses: List[(String, Int)] = List()
  var master: ActorRef = null

  def receive = {
    case Announce(hostname, port) =>
      master = remote.actorFor(
        classOf[MasterService].getCanonicalName,
        hostname,
        port)
      val localhost = remote.address.getHostName()
      val localport = remote.address.getPort()
      master ! Announce(localhost, localport)

    case Nodes(addresses) =>
      println("[ClusterService] received node addresses: " +
              addresses)
      allAddresses = addresses
      self.reply()

    case StartActorAt(_, _, clazz) =>
      println("[ClusterService] starting instance of " + clazz)
      val newActor = actorOf(clazz).start()
      remote.register(newActor)
      newActor ? Nodes(allAddresses)
      self.reply()

    case StopServiceAt(_, _) =>
      println("[ClusterService] shutting down...")
      ClusterService.terminate.countDown()
  }
}
```

Listing 10.9 · The ClusterService actor.

The first thing that might look unfamiliar to you in the previous code is the use of the *at* symbol (@) to prefix the pattern with a chosen identifier (here, startMsg). It works by storing a reference to the message object that matches the pattern in the startMsg variable. We can then use this variable on the right-hand side of the => symbol. This simplifies forwarding the same message unchanged to another actor; in our case, the ClusterService actor returned by nodeRefs((host, port)). After forwarding the StartActorAt message, we use remote.actorFor to obtain an ActorRef to the newly started actor, and send it back as the response.

```
class EchoActor extends Actor {
  var neighbors: List[ActorRef] = List()
  var allAddresses: List[(String, Int)] = List()
  var sum = 0

  def receive = {
    case Nodes(addresses) =>
      allAddresses = addresses
      neighbors = addresses map { case (hostname, port) =>
        remote.actorFor(classOf[ClusterService].getCanonicalName,
          hostname,
          port)
      }
      self.reply()

    case any: String =>
      println("[EchoActor] received " + any)
      // try converting to an Int
      sum += any.toInt
      println("[EchoActor] current sum: " + sum)
  }
}
```

Listing 10.10 · A simple actor that you can start remotely.

Let's test this code. Suppose you'd like to remotely start an instance of the EchoActor class shown in Listing 10.10. This actor responds to two kinds of messages. The first kind of message, with type Nodes, is a message that the cluster service sends right after a new EchoActor instance has been started. As a second kind of message, the actor responds to strings that it converts to integers, which are added to an internal sum.

Starting an EchoActor remotely is pretty simple, given the functionality of the master service:

```
// initialize MasterService
MasterService.main(Array("localhost", "9000", "1"))
// remotely start EchoActor
val response =
  MasterService.master ? StartActorAt("localhost",
                                      9001,
                                      classOf[EchoActor])
val echoActor = response.get.asInstanceOf[ActorRef]
echoActor ! "17"
```

Note that before running the above code you have to start a master service on "localhost:9000" and a cluster service on "localhost:9001". You can terminate the entire "application" as follows:

```
MasterService.master ? StopServiceAt("localhost", 9001)
MasterService.shutdown()
```

In this code, the MasterService instructs a cluster service to shut down by sending it a StopServiceAt message. Upon receiving such a message, the cluster service counts down the terminate latch of its companion object, which causes all actors and the main thread of the cluster service to terminate, as shown in Listing 10.9.

Fault tolerance.   So far, our cluster service is pretty bad at handling faults. For example, let's see what happens if we send an invalid message, such as "hello", to an EchoActor that is started remotely. In this case, the message processing code in EchoActor throws an exception because "hello" cannot be converted to an integer. This unhandled exception leads to output similar to the following:

```
[ERROR]  [8/5/11 3:29 PM] [akka:event-driven:dispatcher:global-5]
  [LocalActorRef] hello
java.lang.NumberFormatException: For input string: "hello"
        at java.lang.NumberFormatException.forInputString(NumberFor
```

```
matException.java:48)
    at java.lang.Integer.parseInt(Integer.java:449)
    at java.lang.Integer.parseInt(Integer.java:499)
```

Moreover, message processing in the EchoActor instance stops. Therefore, your client code can no longer interact with this actor, and may wait for responses indefinitely as a result.

To recover from such unhandled exceptions, Akka provides a powerful mechanism for *actor supervision*. Basically, some actors can play the role of supervisors that are notified whenever a supervised actor crashes. Additionally, supervisors may define fault-handling strategies for recovery by restarting crashed actors.

You can use actor supervision to recover from crashed remote actors by promoting the ClusterService actor to be a supervisor. You can do this in two steps. First, the cluster service actor must link itself to each remote actor that it starts:

```
val newActor = actorOf(clazz)
// start newActor and link to ClusterService
self.startLink(newActor)
remote.register(newActor)
...
```

By linking itself to newActor, the cluster service will be notified when newActor crashes.

Second, the cluster service has to define a fault-handling strategy. You can do this by setting the actor's faultHandler field, for example, in the constructor:

```
self.faultHandler =
  OneForOneStrategy(List(classOf[NumberFormatException],
                    classOf[RuntimeException]), 5, 5000)
```

Akka supports different fault handlers that define different strategies for restarting crashed actors. The simplest strategy restarts the crashed actor (and leaves all other supervised actors alone). The most important parameter of a fault handler is the list of exception types that it handles. In our example, handling NumberFormatException allows you to recover from the case where the EchoActor tries to convert an invalid, non-numeric string to an integer. The other parameters determine the number of restarts that should

143

be attempted, and a timeout within which a restart must be successful (here, 5000 milliseconds).

After setting up the supervisor, you also have to configure the supervised actors—in our case, EchoActor—by defining a life cycle:

```
self.lifeCycle = Permanent
```

The Permanent life cycle configures the supervised actor so that it is always restarted after crashing; the Temporary life cycle configures the supervised actor so that instead of being restarted after crashing, its supervisor terminates it. Moreover, you can clean up the state of the supervised actor by overriding callback methods that are invoked during the termination process.

With this fault-handling mechanism in place, you can recover from the unhandled NumberFormatException caused by a "hello" message:

```
// initialize MasterService
MasterService.main(Array("localhost", "9000", "1"))
// remotely start EchoActor
val response =
  MasterService.master ? StartActorAt("localhost",
                                      9001,
                                      classOf[EchoActor])
val echoActor = response.get.asInstanceOf[ActorRef]
// this will lead to an exception in echoActor
echoActor ! "hello"
// try again; echoActor is restarted automatically
echoActor ! "17"
```

After its crash, the EchoActor resumes message processing, enabling it to handle the 17 message.

Chapter 11

API Overview

This chapter provides a detailed API overview of the `scala.actors` package in Scala 2.8 and Scala 2.9. The organization follows groups of types that logically belong together as well as the trait hierarchy. We focus on the runtime behavior of the various methods that these traits define, thereby complementing the existing Scaladoc-based API documentation.

11.1 The actor traits `Reactor`, `ReplyReactor`, and `Actor`

You can create actors based on several traits that form a simple hierarchy: `Actor <: ReplyReactor <: Reactor` (read "`<:`" as extends). There are two main reasons to prefer using a simpler trait (*i.e.*, a trait further up in the hierarchy) instead of a subtrait:

Types For example, the `Reactor` trait has a type parameter that restricts the type of messages that the trait's instances can receive.

Scalability A `Reactor` (or `ReplyReactor`) maintains fewer instance variables than a `ReplyReactor` (or `Actor`, respectively). This means that an application scales to a larger number of `Reactor`s than `Actor`s, say.

Efficiency The communication primitives that a trait provides are more efficient than those that its supertrait (if any) provides. For example, message sends and `react`s are faster between `Reactor`s than `Actor`s.

The Reactor trait

Reactor is the super-trait of all actor traits. It has a type parameter, Msg, which indicates the type of messages the actor can receive. Extending the Reactor trait allows you to define actors with basic capabilities to send and receive messages.

The behavior of a Reactor is defined by implementing its act method. The act method is executed once the Reactor starts by invoking start, which also returns the Reactor. The start method is *idempotent*, which means that invoking it on an actor that has already been started has no effect.

Invoking the Reactor's (!) method sends a message to the receiver. Sending a message using ! is asynchronous, which means that the sending actor does not wait until the message is received; its execution continues immediately. For example, a ! msg sends msg to a. All actors have a *mailbox*, which buffers incoming messages until they are processed.

The Reactor trait also defines a forward method. This method is inherited from OutputChannel. It has the same effect as the ! method. Subtraits of Reactor, in particular the ReplyReactor trait, override this method to enable implicit reply destinations. This will be described in the next section of this chapter.

A Reactor receives messages using the react method.[1] react expects an argument of type PartialFunction[Msg, Unit], which defines how messages of type Msg are handled once they arrive in the actor's mailbox. In the following example, the current actor waits to receive the string "Hello", and then prints a greeting:

```
react {
  case "Hello" =>
    println("Hi there")
}
```

The react method never returns. Therefore, any code that should run after a message has been received must be contained inside the partial function that is passed to react. For example, two messages can be received in sequence by nesting two invocations of react:

---

[1] By default, this method does not show up in the ScalaDoc API documentation, because its visibility is protected[actors]. This can be changed by selecting visibility "All" on the ScalaDoc page.

```
react {
  case Get(from) =>
    react {
      case Put(x) => from ! x
    }
}
```

The Reactor trait also provides control structures, which simplify programming with react. These control structures will be described in Section 11.2.

Termination and execution states

A Reactor's execution terminates when the body of its act method has run to completion. A Reactor can also terminate itself explicitly using the exit method. The return type of exit is Nothing, because exit always throws an exception. This exception is only used internally, and should never be caught by user code.

You can restart a terminated Reactor by invoking its restart method. Invoking restart on a Reactor that has not terminated yet will produce an IllegalStateException. Restarting a terminated actor causes its act method to rerun.

Reactor defines a method getState, which returns the actor's current execution state as a member of the Actor.State enumeration. An actor that has not been started yet is in state Actor.State.New. An actor that can run without waiting for a message is in state Actor.State.Runnable. An actor that is suspended, *i.e.*, waiting for a message, is in execution state Actor.State.Suspended. An actor that is terminated is in execution state Actor.State.Terminated.

Exception handling

The exceptionHandler member allows you to define an exception handler that is enabled throughout a Reactor's lifetime:

```
def exceptionHandler: PartialFunction[Exception, Unit]
```

You use the partial function returned from exceptionHandler to handle exceptions that are not otherwise handled: whenever an exception propagates

147

from the body of a Reactor's act method, the partial function is applied to that exception, allowing the actor to run clean-up code before it terminates.[2]

Handling exceptions using exceptionHandler works well together with the control structures for programming with react, which will be covered in Section 11.2. Whenever an exception has been handled using the partial function returned by exceptionHandler, execution continues with the current continuation closure. For example, imagine an exception is thrown by this code:

```
loop {
  react {
    case Msg(data) =>
      if (cond) // process data
      else throw new Exception("cannot process data")
  }
}
```

Assuming that the Reactor overrides exceptionHandler, after the exception thrown inside the body of react is handled, execution will continue with the next loop iteration.

The ReplyReactor trait

The ReplyReactor trait extends Reactor[Any] and adds or overrides the following methods:

The ! method (overridden) obtains a reference to the current actor, *i.e.*, the sender; together with the actual message, the sender reference is transferred to the receiving actor's mailbox. The receiver has access to the message's sender via the sender method.

The forward method (overridden) obtains a reference to the *sender* of the message that is currently being processed. Together with the actual message, this reference is transferred as the current message's sender. As a consequence, forward enables the forwarding of messages on behalf of actors different from the current actor.

---

[2]Note that the visibility of exceptionHandler is protected.

148

The sender method (added) returns the sender of the message currently being processed. Given that a message may have been forwarded, sender may not return the actor that actually sent the message.

The reply method (added) sends a message back to the most recently handled message's sender. reply is also used to reply to a synchronous message send (via !?) or a message send with a future (via !!).

The !? methods (added) provide *synchronous message sends*. Invoking !? causes the sending actor to wait until a response is received, which is then returned. There are two overloaded variants. In addition, the two-parameter variant takes a timeout argument (in milliseconds), and its return type is Option[Any] instead of Any. If the sender does not receive a response within the specified timeout period, !? returns None; otherwise, it returns the response wrapped in Some.

The !! methods (added) are similar to the synchronous message sends provided by !? in that they allow transferring a response from the receiver. However, instead of blocking the sending actor until a response is received, they return Future instances. You can use a Future to retrieve the response of the receiver once it is available; you can also use it to find out whether the response is already available without blocking the sender. There are two overloaded variants of the !! method. The two-parameter variant takes an argument of type PartialFunction[Any, A]. This partial function is used for post-processing the receiver's response. Essentially, !! returns a future that applies the partial function to the response once it is received. The result of the future is the result of this post-processing step.

The reactWithin method (added) allows you to receive messages within a given period of time. Compared to react, it takes an additional parameter, msec, which indicates the time period in milliseconds until the special TIMEOUT pattern matches (TIMEOUT is a case object in the scala.actors package).. Here's an example:

```
reactWithin(2000) {
  case Answer(text) => // process text
  case TIMEOUT => println("no answer within 2 seconds")
}
```

149

The `reactWithin` method also allows non-blocking access to the mailbox. When specifying a time period of 0 milliseconds, the mailbox is first scanned to find a matching message. If there is no matching message after the first scan, the TIMEOUT pattern matches. One use case for 0 timeouts is to enable receiving certain messages with a higher priority than others:

```
reactWithin(0) {
  case HighPriorityMsg => // ...
  case TIMEOUT =>
    react {
      case LowPriorityMsg => // ...
    }
}
```

In this example, the actor first processes the next HighPriorityMsg, even if there is a LowPriorityMsg that arrived earlier in its mailbox. The actor only processes a LowPriorityMsg *first* if there is no HighPriorityMsg in its mailbox.

The ReplyReactor trait adds the `Actor.State.TimedSuspended` execution state. An actor that is suspended, waiting to receive a message using `reactWithin`, is in state `Actor.State.TimedSuspended`.

The Actor trait

The Actor trait extends `ReplyReactor` and adds the following members:

The receive method (added) behaves like `react` except that it may return a result. This is reflected in its type signature, which is polymorphic in its result type:

```
def receive[R](f: PartialFunction[Any, R]): R
```

However, using `receive` makes the actor more heavyweight, since `receive` blocks the underlying thread while the actor is suspended waiting for a message. The blocked thread is unavailable to execute other actors until the invocation of `receive` returns.

The link and unlink methods (added) allow an actor to link and unlink itself to and from another actor, respectively. You can use linking for monitoring and reacting to the termination of another actor. In particular, linking affects the behavior of invoking exit, as explained in the Actor trait's API documentation.

The trapExit member (added) allows an actor to react to the termination of linked actors independently of the exit reason (that is, it does not matter whether the exit reason is 'normal or not). If an actor's trapExit member is set to true, this actor will never terminate because of linked actors. Instead, whenever one of its linked actors terminates it will receive a message of type Exit. The Exit case class has two members: from refers to the actor that terminated; reason refers to the exit reason.

Termination and execution states

When terminating the execution of an Actor instance, the exit reason can be set explicitly by invoking the following variant of exit:

```
def exit(reason: AnyRef): Nothing
```

An actor that terminates with an exit reason different from 'normal (the symbol) propagates its exit reason to all actors linked to it. If an actor terminates because of an uncaught exception, its exit reason is an instance of the UncaughtException case class.

The Actor trait adds two new execution states. An actor waiting to receive a message using receive is in state Actor.State.Blocked. An actor waiting to receive a message using receiveWithin—*i.e.*, waiting with a timeout—is in state Actor.State.TimedBlocked.

11.2 Control structures

The Reactor trait defines control structures that simplify programming with the non-returning react operation. Normally, an invocation of react does not return. If the actor should execute code subsequently, you can either pass the actor's continuation code explicitly to react, or use one of the control structures, described in this section, which hide these continuations.

The most basic control structure is andThen. It allows you to register a closure that is executed once the actor has finished executing everything else. For example, the actor shown in Listing 11.1 prints a greeting after it has processed the "hello" message. Even though the invocation of react does

```
actor {
  {
    react {
      case "hello" => // processing "hello"
    }: Unit
  } andThen {
    println("hi there")
  }
}
```

Listing 11.1 · Using andThen for sequencing.

not return, you can use andThen to register the code that prints the greeting as the actor's continuation.

Note that there is a *type ascription*, ": Unit," that follows the react invocation. This essentially allows you to treat the result of react as having type Unit, which is legal since the result of any expression can always be converted to Unit. This is necessary since andThen cannot be a member of type Nothing, which is the result type of react. Treating the result type of react as Unit enables the application of an implicit conversion that makes the andThen member available.

The API provides a few more control structures:

loop { ... } Loops indefinitely, executing the code in braces each iteration. Invoking react inside the loop body causes the actor to react to a message as usual. Subsequently, execution continues with the next iteration of the same loop.

loopWhile (c) { ... } Executes the code in braces while the condition c returns true. Invoking react in the loop body has the same effect as in the case of loop.

continue Continues with the execution of the current continuation closure. Invoking continue inside the body of a loop or loopWhile will cause the actor to finish the current iteration and continue with the next iteration. If the current continuation has been registered using andThen, execution will continue with the closure passed as the second argument to andThen.

152

You can use the control structures anywhere in the body of a Reactor's act method and in the bodies of methods transitively called by act. For actors created using the actor { ... } shorthand, the control structures can be imported from the Actor object.

11.3 Futures

The ReplyReactor and Actor traits support result-bearing message send operations (the !! methods) that immediately return a *future*. A future, an instance of the Future trait, is a handle you can use to retrieve the response to a *send-with-future* message.

The sender of a send-with-future message can wait for the future's response by *applying* the future. For example, using val fut = a !! msg to send a message allows the sender to wait for the result of the future as follows: val res = fut(). In addition, a Future can be queried using the isSet method to find out whether its result is available without blocking.

A send-with-future message is not the only way to obtain a future. You can create futures from computations using the future method. In the following example, we start the computation body to run concurrently, returning a future for its result:

```
val fut = future { body }
// ...
fut() // wait for future
```

What makes futures special in the context of actors is the possibility to retrieve their result using the standard actor-based receive operations, such as receive. Moreover, you can use the event-based operations react and reactWithin. This enables an actor to wait for the result of a future without blocking its underlying thread.

The actor-based receive operations are made available through the future's inputChannel. For a future of type Future[T], its input channel type is InputChannel[T]; for example:

```
val fut = a !! msg
// ...
fut.inputChannel.react {
  case Response => // ...
}
```

11.4 Channels

You can use channels to simplify the handling of messages that have different types but are sent to the same actor. The hierarchy of channels is divided into OutputChannels and InputChannels.

OutputChannels can be sent messages. An OutputChannel, out, supports the following operations:

out ! msg Asynchronously sends msg to out. A reference to the sending actor is transferred, as in the case where msg is sent directly to an actor.

out forward msg Asynchronously forwards msg to out. The sending actor is determined, as in the case where msg is forwarded directly to an actor.

out.receiver Returns the unique actor that is receiving messages sent to the out channel.

out.send(msg, from) Asynchronously sends msg to out supplying from as the sender of the message.

The OutputChannel trait has a type parameter that specifies the type of messages that can be sent to the channel using !, forward, and send. The type parameter is contravariant.

Actors can receive messages from InputChannels. Like its sibling, OutputChannel, the InputChannel trait has a type parameter that specifies the type of messages that can be received from the channel, but this type parameter is covariant. An InputChannel[Msg] (named in) supports the following operations:

in.receive { case Pat1 => ... ; case Pat2 => ... ; ...} Receives a message from in. Invoking receive on an input channel has the same semantics as the standard receive operation for actors. The only difference is that the partial function passed as an argument has type PartialFunction[Msg, R], where R is the return type of receive.

154

in.receiveWithin { case Pat1 => ... ; case Pat2 => ... ; ... } Same as receive, but with a timeout.

in.react { case Pat1 => ... ; case Pat2 => ... ; ... } Receives, using an event-based react operation, a message from in. Like react for actors, the return type is Nothing, indicating that invocations of this method never return. Like the receive operation on InputChannel, the partial function passed as an argument has a more specific type: PartialFunction[Msg, Unit].

in.reactWithin { case Pat1 => ... ; case Pat2 => ... ; ... } Same as react, but with a timeout.

Creating and sharing channels

Channels are created using the concrete Channel class. It extends both InputChannel and OutputChannel. A channel can be shared either by making the channel visible in the scopes of multiple actors, or by sending it in a message.

```
actor {
  var out: OutputChannel[String] = null
  val child = actor {
    react {
      case "go" => out ! "hello"
    }
  }
  val channel = new Channel[String]
  out = channel
  child ! "go"
  channel.receive {
    case msg => println(msg.length)
  }
}
```

Listing 11.2 · Scope-based sharing of channels.

The example in Listing 11.2 demonstrates scope-based sharing. Running this example prints the string "5" to the console. Note that the child actor has

155

only access to out, which is an OutputChannel[String]. The channel
reference, which can also be used to receive messages, is hidden. However,
care must be taken to ensure the output channel is initialized to a concrete
channel before the child sends messages to it. This is done using the "go"
message. When receiving from channel using channel.receive, we can
make use of the fact that msg is of type String; therefore, it provides a
length member.

```scala
case class ReplyTo(out: OutputChannel[String])
val child = actor {
  react {
    case ReplyTo(out) => out ! "hello"
  }
}
actor {
  val channel = new Channel[String]
  child ! ReplyTo(channel)
  channel.receive {
    case msg => println(msg.length)
  }
}
```

Listing 11.3 · Sharing channels via messages.

An alternative way to share channels is by sending them in messages, as
the example in Listing 11.3 demonstrates. The ReplyTo case class is a message type we use to distribute a reference to an OutputChannel[String].
When the child actor receives a ReplyTo message, it sends a string to its
output channel. The second actor receives a message on that channel, as it
did in the previous example shown in Listing 11.2.

11.5 Remote Actors API

This section describes Scala's remote actors API. Its main interface is the
RemoteActor object in package scala.actors.remote. This object provides methods to create and connect to remote actor instances. In the code

snippets below, we assume that all members of RemoteActor have been imported; the full list of imports that we use is as follows:

```
import scala.actors._
import scala.actors.Actor._
import scala.actors.remote._
import scala.actors.remote.RemoteActor._
```

Starting remote actors

A remote actor is uniquely identified by a Symbol. This symbol is unique to the JVM instance on which the remote actor is executed. A remote actor identified with name 'myActor can be created as follows:

```
class MyActor extends Actor {
  def act() {
    alive(9000)
    register('myActor, self)
    // ...
  }
}
```

Note that a name can only be registered with a single (alive) actor at a time. For example, to register an actor A as 'myActor, and then register another actor B as 'myActor, you would first have to wait until A terminated. This requirement applies across all ports on a single JVM, so simply registering B on a different port as A is not sufficient.

Connecting to remote actors

Connecting to a remote actor is just as simple. To obtain a remote reference to a remote actor running on machine myMachine on port 8000 with name 'anActor, use select in the following manner:

```
val myRemoteActor = select(Node("myMachine", 8000), 'anActor)
```

The actor returned from select has type AbstractActor, which provides essentially the same interface as a regular actor, and thus supports the usual message send operations:

```
myRemoteActor ! "Hello!"
receive {
  case response => println("Response: " + response)
}
myRemoteActor !? "What is the meaning of life?" match {
  case 42   => println("Success")
  case oops => println("Failed: " + oops)
}
val future = myRemoteActor !! "What is the last digit of PI?"
```

Note that the `select` method is lazy; it does not actually initiate any network connections. It simply creates a new `AbstractActor` instance, which is ready to initiate a new network connection when needed (for instance, when !! is invoked).

Bibliography

[Agh90] Agha, Gul. "Concurrent Object-Oriented Programming." *Communications of the ACM*, 33(9):125–141, September 1990.

[Arm95] Armstrong, J. L., M. C. Williams, C. Wikström, and S. R. Virding. *Concurrent Programming in Erlang*. Prentice Hall, second edition, 1995.

[Dea08] Dean, Jeffrey and Sanjay Ghemawat. "MapReduce: simplified data processing on large clusters." *CACM*, 51(1):107–113, 2008.

[Goe06] Goetz, Brian, Tim Peierls, Joshua Bloch, Joseph Bowbeer, David Holmes, and Doug Lea. *Java Concurrency in Practice*. Addison Wesley, 2006. ISBN 978-0321349606.

[Gro99] Gropp, William, Ewing Lusk, and Anthony Skjellum. *Using MPI: Portable Parallel Programming with the Message–Passing Interface*. The MIT Press, Cambridge, MA, second edition, 1999.

[Hal09] Haller, Philipp and Martin Odersky. "Scala Actors: Unifying Thread-based and Event-based Programming." *Theor. Comput. Sci*, 410(2-3):202–220, 2009.

[Hal10] Haller, Philipp and Martin Odersky. "Capabilities for Uniqueness and Borrowing." In *Proceedings of the 24th European Conference on Object-Oriented Programming (ECOOP'10)*, pages 354–378. Springer, June 2010. ISBN 978-3-642-14106-5.

[HB77] Henry Baker, Carl Hewitt. "Laws for Communicating Parallel Processes." Technical report, MIT Artificial Intelligence Laboratory, http://hdl.handle.net/1721.1/41962, 1977.

[Hen11] Hennessy, John L. and David A. Patterson. *Computer Architecture: A Quantitative Approach, 5th Edition*. Morgan Kaufmann, 2011. ISBN 978-0123838728.

[Hew73] Hewitt, Carl, Peter Bishop, and Richard Steiger. "A Universal Modular ACTOR Formalism for Artificial Intelligence." In *Proceedings of the Third International Joint Conference on Artificial Intelligence (IJCAI'73)*, pages 235–245. 1973.

[Hew77] Hewitt, Carl E. "Viewing Control Structures as Patterns of Passing Messages." *Journal of Artificial Intelligence*, 8(3):323–364, 1977.

[Hoa78] Hoare, C. A. R. "Communicating Sequential Processes." *Comm.ACM*, 21(8):666–677, 1978.

[Kay98] Kay, Alan. an email on messaging in Smalltalk/Squeak, 1998. The email is published on the web at http://lists.squeakfoundation.org/pipermail/squeak-dev/1998-October/017019.html.

[Sut05] Sutter, Herb. "The Free Lunch Is Over: A Fundamental Turn Toward Concurrency." *Dr. Dobb's Journal*, March 2005.

About the Authors

Philipp Haller

Philipp Haller is a post-doctoral researcher at Stanford University, USA, and at EPFL, Switzerland. He holds a Dipl.-Inform. degree from Karlsruhe Institute of Technology, Germany, and a Ph.D. in Computer Science from EPFL, Switzerland. As a member of the Scala team at EPFL he has been working on programming abstractions for concurrency, as well as type systems to check their safety. Philipp created Scala Actors, a library for efficient, high-level concurrent programming.

Frank Sommers

Frank Sommers is president of Autospaces, Inc., a company specializing in automotive finance software. After almost 15 years of working with Java, Frank started programming in Scala a few years ago, and became an instant fan of the language. Frank is an active writer in the area of information technology and computing. His main interests are parallel and distributed computing, data management, programming languages, cluster and cloud computing, open-source software, and online user communities.

Index

Page numbers followed by an n *refer to footnotes.*

Symbols

! (asynchronous message send)
  defined by `ScalaActorRef` trait, 127
  in Akka actors, 127
  on trait `Actor`, 49–50
  on trait `Reactor`, 146

(!) (asynchronous message send)
  in Erlang actors, 49

!! (futures message send)
  on trait `Actor`, 52, 149, 153
  on trait `ReplyReactor`, 149

!? (synchronous message send)
  on trait `Actor`, 50–51
  on trait `ReplyReactor`, 149

? (synchronous message send)
  in Akka actors, 136

A

activation events, 25

`Actor` trait
  in Akka, 125
  in Scala, 145, 153

actor-based programming
  defining message classes, 46
  messages altering
    internal state, 46
    subsequent behavior, 46
  with Scala, 4

`actorOf` method, in Akka
  on object `Actor`, 127

`ActorRef` trait, in Akka
  implicitly converted to
    `ScalaActorRef` trait, 125

actors
  Akka vs. Scala, 133
  and event dispatch threads, 89
  and Swing, 89
  and thread-bound properties,
    86–89
  child, 24
  concepts, 24–26
  creating vs. starting, 30
  daemon-style, 90
  definition of, 19
  designing with, 21
  distributed, *see* actors, remote
  DSL, 45
  event-based versus
    thread-based, 55–56
  events, concept of, 24–26
  late binding of, 22–23
  life cycle of, 30
  local vs. remote, 27
  model, 3, 24–26
  remote, 101–104, 135, 156–158
    Akka, 135–144
    connecting to, 157
    creating, 157
    linking, 104
    starting, 157

starting vs. creating, 30
states, *see* states, actor
theory of, 24–26
versus threads, 5–8
actors.corePoolSize, 59
actors.maxPoolSize, 59
AJAX, 27
Akka, 125–144
  ! (asynchronous message send)
    defined by ScalaActorRef
      trait, 127
  ? (synchronous message send)
    in Akka actors, 136
  accessing actors, 128
  Actor trait, 125
  actorOf method
    on object Actor, 127
  ActorRef trait, 125–128, 136
    implicitly converted to
      ScalaActorRef trait, 127
  actors
    Akka vs. Scala, 133
  become method
    on trait Actor, 130, 131, 133
  creating actors, 125–129
  fault tolerance, 142–144
  forward method
    on trait ScalaActorRef, 127
  message handling, 129–134
    unhandled messages,
      131–134
    UnhandledMessageException,
      132
  monitoring actors, 143
  parallel processing example,
    130–131
  receive method
    on trait Akka Actor, 127
  remote actors, 135–144
  reply method
    on trait ScalaActorRef, 127

shutting down actors, 126, 138,
  142
start method
  on trait Actor, 126
starting actors, 126, 135, 142
supervision, of actors, 143
andThen method
  on trait Reactor, 151
arbiter, 28
  concept of, 29
arrival events, 25
asynchronous message sends (!)
  defined by ScalaActorRef
    trait, 127
  in Akka actors, 127
  in Erlang actors, 49
  on trait Actor, 49–50
  on trait Reactor, 146
asynchronous messaging, 27

B
Baker, Henry, 25
become method, in Akka
  on trait Actor, 130, 131, 133
Blocked, actor state, 151
broadcast, reliable, 118–124
by-name parameters, 84
  Scala, basic concepts of, 36, 38

C
"Capabilities for Uniqueness and
  Borrowing" (Haller and
  Odersky), 6n
case statement, *see* pattern matching
chaining methods
  Scala, basic concepts of, 39
channels, 154–156
  creating, 155
  InputChannel trait, 154
  OutputChannel trait, 154
  sharing, 155–156
chat application, 46
ChatRoom, 46

checked exceptions
Scala, basic concepts of, 34
child actors, 24
closures, 63, 64, 89
combining control structures
Scala, basic concepts of, 39
"Communicating Sequential
Processes" (Hoare), 5n, 9n
*Computer Architecture: A
Quantitative Approach*
(Hennessy and Patterson),
7n
"Concurrent Object-Oriented
Programming" (Agha),
20n
Concurrent Programming in Erlang
(Armstrong, *et al.*), 5n
continuation-passing style (CPS), 20
continuations, 20–23
continue method
on trait Reactor, 152
control-flow
concept of, 15–19
continue method on trait
Reactor, 152
loop method on trait Reactor,
152
loopWhile method on trait
Reactor, 152
of react-based actors, 63
andThen method on object
Actor, 63
building custom operators, 66
loopWhile method on object
Actor, 64
creating
remote actors, 157
creating actors
in Akka, 125–129
vs. starting, 30
creating control structures, Scala,
basic concepts of, 36

currying
Scala, basic concepts of, 39–40

D

daemon-style actors, 90
data-flow, concept of, 15–19
Dean, Jeffrey, 108
defining control structures, Scala,
basic concepts of, 39
denial-of-service, 28
determinism, and actor model, 13
deterministic actor execution, 90–98
differences between Scala and Akka
actors
message reception semantics,
133
sending messages from outside
actors, 129
division-of-labor tenet
Scala, basic concepts of, 39
domain specific language (DSL), 45
downloading
source code for book examples,
xxv

E

Erlang language, xvii
errata, viewing and reporting, xxv
error handling, 74
event dispatch threads, 89
events
activation, 25
actor model, 25
arrival, 25
example code, for book
downloading, xxv
license of, xxv
exception handling, 71–74
futures, 84
Exit class, 78, 151
exit method
on trait Reactor, 147

F

fault tolerance, 74, 107, 115
    in Akka, 142–144
fork-join parallelism, 24
forward method
    in Akka, on trait
        ScalaActorRef, 127
    on trait Reactor, 146
    on trait ReplyReactor, 148
"The Free lunch Is Over: A
    Fundamental Turn Toward
    Concurrency, The"
    (Sutter), 4n
functions
    first-class objects, Scala, basic
        concepts of, 35
    literals, Scala, basic concepts
        of, 35
future method
    on trait Future, 153
futures, 153–154
    concept of, 52
    construct of, 153
    event-based, 65–69
    exception handling, 84
    isSet method
        on trait Future, 153
    send-with-future message, 153
futures message sends (!!)
    on trait Actor, 52, 149, 153
    on trait ReplyReactor, 149

G

getState method
    on trait Reactor, 147
Ghemawat, Sanjay, 108
Google protocol buffers, 135
graceful shutdown
    actors, in Akka, 126

H

Hewitt, Carl, 3, 25

I

incoming message processing
    pattern matching, 43
indeterminism, unbounded, 13, 29
index, inverted, 108
inferring
    method return types, Scala,
        basic concepts of, 33
    variable types, Scala, basic
        concepts of, 33
isSet method
    on trait Future, 153

J

Java Concurrency in Practice (Goetz
    et al.), 5n
Java Native Interface (JNI), 89

K

Kay, Alan, 23n, 23

L

late binding, of actors, 22–23
"Laws for Communicating Parallel
    Processes" (Hewitt and
    Baker), 25n
life cycle of actors, 30
link method
    on trait Actor, 151
linking actors, 76–80, 150
    remote, 104

M

mailbox, 28
    concept of, 29
managed blocking, 94–99
MapReduce, 12–13
"MapReduce: Simplified Data
    Processing on Large
    Clusters" (Dean and
    Ghemawat), 12n, 107n
message delays, 27
message handling

in Akka, 129–134
    unhandled messages, in Akka,
        131–134
    UnhandledMessageException
        in Akka, 132
message processing, 45–53
    behaviors, Scala, basic concepts
        of, 39
    defining act method, 47
    invoking start, 47
    obtaining next available
        message, 47
monitoring actors, 30, 74–84, 150
    in Akka, 143
Moore's Law
    applied to computing
        performance, 4

O

Oz language, xvii

P

parallel hardware, 4
pattern matching
    incoming message processing,
        43
    Scala, basic concepts of, 42–43
"poison pill", 30
principles of
    locality, 18
    "send it and forget it", 27
pthreads library, xvii

R

race conditions
    avoided by design, 6
react and receive
    differences, 56–69
react method, 146–148
    on trait Future, 153
Reactor trait, 145–148
    andThen control flow, 151
    continue control flow, 152

control flow, 153
    loop control flow, 152
    loopWhile control flow, 152
reactWithin method
    on trait Future, 153
    on trait ReplyReactor, 149
receive method
    in Akka on trait Akka Actor,
        127
    on trait Actor, 150
receiveWithin method
    on trait Actor, 53
recursion
    with react method, 60
register method
    on class RemoteActor, 101
reliable broadcast, 118–124
remote actors, 101–104, 156–158
    Akka, 135–144
    connecting to, 157
    creating, 157
    linking, 104
    local vs remote, 27
    starting, 157
reply method
    in Akka, on trait
        ScalaActorRef, 127
    on trait ReplyReactor, 149
ReplyReactor trait, 145, 148–150,
    153
restart method
    on trait Reactor, 147

S

"Scala Actors: Unifying
    Thread-based and
    Event-based
    Programming" (Haller and
    Odersky), 3n
Scala, basic concepts of
    by-name parameters, 36, 38
    chaining methods, 39
    checked exceptions, 34

combining control structures, 39

creating control structures, 36

currying, 39–40

defining control structures, 39

division-of-labor tenet, 39

favoring immutable data structures, 33

first-class functions, 35

function literals, 35

functions as control structures, 36–39

generalizing control flow, 41

inferring method return types, 33

inferring variable types, 33

message sending and processing behaviors, 39

pattern matching, 42–43

scaling via concurrency, 33

structural typing, 41

ScalaActorRef trait

in Akka, implicitly converted to, 125

SchedulerAdapter trait, 89

schedulers

customizing, 85–94

select method

on classRemoteActor, 103

"send it and forget it", 27

send-with-future message, 153

sender method

on trait ReplyReactor, 149

Shirley Temple, *see* child actors

shutting down actors

in Akka, 126, 138, 142

SingleThreadedScheduler, 94

Smalltalk, 23n

Squeak, 23n

starting actors

in Akka, 126, 135, 142

vs. creating, 30

starting remote actors, 157

states, actor

Blocked, 151

New, 147

Runnable, 147

Suspended, 74, 147

Terminated, 74, 147

TimedBlocked, 151

structural typing

Scala, basic concepts of, 41

supervision, of actors

in Akka, 143

Swing, using actors with, 89

switch statement, *see* pattern matching

synchronous message sends

!?

on trait Actor, 50–51

on trait ReplyReactor, 149

?

in Akka actors, 136

T

terminating actors, 26, 30, 56–58, 60, 61, 75

automatically, 71

exit reason, 77

propagating exit reason, 151

trapping, 78–84

thread-bound properties, 86–89

thread-per-actor approach, 55

time, local vs. global, 26

TimedBlocked, actor state, 151

TimedSuspended state

on trait ReplyReactor, 150

tips and techniques

react plays extremely well with recursive methods, 61

a name can only be registered with a single (alive) actor at a time. This requirement applies across all ports on a single JVM, 157

Akka requires message handlers
to handle *all message types*
that are possibly sent to the
actor, 133
Code surrounding an invocation
of `react` should never
catch instances of
`java.lang.Throwable`,
60
In Akka, most of the actor API
is accessed through
`ActorRefs`, 126
in some cases, actors can use a
mix of event-based code
and thread-based code, 94
Invoking `react` must always be
the last thing an
event-based actor does
before it terminates, 60
Once an actor has exceeded its
useful life, it can be
stopped and destroyed,
either of its own accord, or
as a result of some "poison
pill", 30
operations that may block the
underlying thread have to
be used with care, so as to
avoid locking up the entire
thread pool, 95
some messages sent to an actor
can alter the actor's
internal state, 46
You would almost always want
to define your actor
messages as Scala case
classes, 43
`trapExit` member
in trait `Actor`, 151

unhandled messages, in Akka,
131–134
`UnhandledMessageException`, in
Akka, 132
"Universal Modular ACTOR
Formalism for Artificial
Intelligence, A" (Hewitt *et
al.*), 3n
`unlink` method
on trait `Actor`, 151
*Using MPI: Portable Parallel
Programming with the
Message–Passing
Interface* (Gropp *et al.*), 5n

U

unbounded indeterminism, 13, 29

Stairway to Scala Workshop

from Escalate Software

www.escalatesoft.com

If you've decided to use Scala, and want to speed up the time it takes to get proficient and productive, then Escalate Software's *Stairway to Scala Workshop* is for you. The course, which is divided into *applied* and *advanced* parts, is designed to save you time in your transition to Scala.

Stairway to Scala Applied, a three-day course of Scala fundamentals, will take you step-by-step through the most important aspects of the Scala language and API, as well as the important ideas behind them. At each step, you'll gain a deeper understanding of Scala's design and how Scala can help you accomplish a wide range of practical programming tasks, from writing small scripts to building large systems. After taking this course you'll be able to code in Scala with confidence, and enjoy the productivity boost the Scala promises to those who master it.

If you feel you have reached a level of proficiency in Scala but want to take your Scala programming to the next level, then *Stairway to Scala Advanced* is for you. This two-day course will take you through many advanced topics, including actors, and at each step you will gain a deeper understanding of Scala's advanced features and how you can apply them in the real world. If you already use Scala regularly, this course will make you more productive and able to tackle tougher challenges.

For information on Escalate Software's next public Scala workshops, visit:

`http://www.escalatesoft.com/training`

Other titles from Artima Press

Hiring software professionals is difficult, but few books exist on this specific topic. *Agile Hiring* presents a fresh approach that is tested by fire: developed by the author in over twenty years of experience hiring software professionals at both small companies and large. Drawing on principles from the "agile" software movement, this book offers a different way to think about hiring. This book provides principles and techniques that will help you hire the best software professionals.

Agile Hiring: Transform how you hire software professionals
by Sean Landis
ISBN: 978-0-9815316-3-2
$29.95 paper book / $20.00 PDF eBook
Order it now at: `http://www.artima.com/shop/agile_hiring`

Flex 4 Fun is the authoritative guide to graphics and animation in Flex 4: the fun stuff! The book is filled with insightful tips on user interface programming and includes nearly seventy example programs written expressly for the book. Written by Chet Haase, an engineer on the Flex SDK team at Adobe during the development of Flex 4 and coauthor of *Filthy Rich Clients*, this book will teach you the graphical and animation side of Flex 4 that enable better user experiences.

Flex 4 Fun: Graphics and animation for better user interfaces
by Chet Haase
ISBN: 978-0-9815316-2-5
$36.95 paper book / $23.00 PDF eBook
Order it now at: `http://www.artima.com/shop/flex_4_fun`

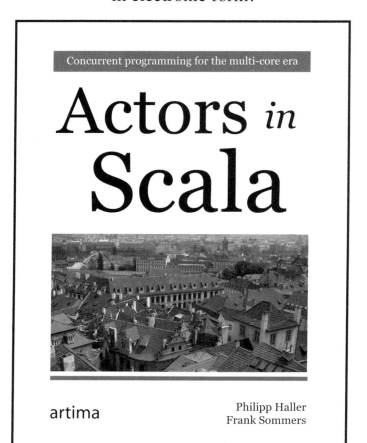